W9-BDF-231

From The Great Omission to Vibrant Faith

The Role of the Home in Renewing the Church

David W. Anderson

VFP

Vibrant Faith Publishing
by
The Youth & Family Institute

FROM THE GREAT OMISSION TO VIBRANT FAITH
The Role of the Home in Renewing the Church

Copyright © 2009 The Youth & Family Institute. All rights reserved. Except for brief quotations in critical articles or reviews, no part of this book may be reproduced in any manner without prior written permission from the publisher.

Scripture quotations are from the New Revised Standard Version Bible, copyright © 1989 by the Division of Christian Education of the National Council of the Churches of Christ in the USA. All rights reserved.

Cover images © iStockphoto. Used by permission.
Cover and book design: Jessica Hillstrom, Hillspring Books

Library of Congress Cataloging-in-Publication Data
ISBN 978-1-889407-48-7

The paper used in this publication meets the minimum requirements of American National Standard for Information Sciences—Permanence of Paper for Printed Library Materials, ANSI Z329.48-1984. Manufactured in the U.S.A.

14 13 12 11 10 09 1 2 3 4 5 6 7 8 9 10

CONTENTS

SERIES FOREWORD

It is difficult to be a parent these days. It is difficult to be a church leader as well. The challenges they both face are enormous. And the challenges they both face are the same, although they may not recognize this fact. The challenge is to address these questions: "How do I live a vibrant faith, and what are effective practices for helping my children and others live a vibrant faith?"

Whereas church leaders may understand this question, most parents probably do not. It is not their fault. Over the past fifty years, the church—understood as the congregation and its leaders—has not put this question to parents or taught them how to do it. Rather, by accident or mutual quiet consent, parents and church leaders agreed to a solution that does not work: Let the congregational leaders be responsible to engrain children and members with vibrant faith. The results have been disastrous. Young people, while often remaining spiritual, have left congregational life in droves. Parents are less equipped and feel inadequate to discuss matters of faith. And church leaders, having tried every experiment and practice they can imagine, feel frustrated and struggle with their own sense of low morale.

This is the situation much of the church finds itself in today. It is to this situation that my friend and colleague Dr. David Anderson writes. This book identifies a repeated mistake in church practices all across North America. The mistake is not inviting, equipping, and expecting parents and other adults to play a vital role in their own faith formation and that of their children and the young. Anderson calls this error *the great omission*.

This book is about how to approach this dilemma of the church. David Anderson brings more than twenty years experience of researching, speaking, consulting, writing, and coaching individuals, parents, and congregations in the effective practices of vibrant faith formation. Few scholars bring the breadth and depth of knowledge and experience relating to this issue as he does.

I know this from personal experience. In 2004, David and I co-wrote a book with the strange title *Frogs without Legs Can't Hear*. In that book we laid out the theological, confessional, and research case for why it is important that homes be considered church too. We told lots of stories, most of them at our own expense, and we offered ideas and practical steps for how to equip homes for faith formation. It was a book somewhat on the cutting edge, and we are now pretty convinced not everyone was ready to hear what we had to say.

The times have changed indeed. At The Youth & Family Institute, we have assembled more than thirty years of research from a wide variety of sources. And it all says basically the same thing. Home and family life is the primary incubator for faith formation. Secular studies, such as *Hardwired to Connect* done in 2003, lift up the important role of spiritual adults in the moral and spiritual formation of children. Christian Smith and his team from the University of North Carolina, in the largest study ever done of adolescent spirituality, states in his book *SoulSearching* that "we'll get what we are." In other words, there is no generation gap, as Margaret Meade spoke of in the 1960s. For the most part parents are the primary influence in the moral and spiritual shaping of their children.

Innumerable religious studies point out the important role parents and adults play in the vibrant faith formation of their children. Barna Research stated in 2003 that families, not congregations, need to take the lead in the spiritual development of their children. The Exemplary Practices Research done by a team representing seven denominations identified five ways in which families and homes play a critical role in faith formation. And most recently, both the SEARCH Institute (secular) and the Center for Ministry Development (Roman

Catholic) have presented new research representing many countries and continents that illustrates the central role homes and families play in the spiritual development of children and youth.

Much has changed since David and I wrote "the Frogs book." Yet much has not. Whereas the research keeps affirming the premise we made in that book, actual change in congregational and parental practices are slow to develop.

Therefore, David Anderson is writing a three-volume set on effective practices in vibrant faith formation. These volumes represent the launch of Vibrant Faith Publishing resources from The Youth & Family Institute. This first book is written for congregational leaders. It offers new ways to think about congregational leadership with vibrant faith formation being the thrust of that effort. Volume two will address congregational practices such as worship and Christian education. Volume three will speak directly to parents and other adults regarding vibrant faith practices in their own lives and that of their children.

Anderson's work provides much of the backbone to what we do at The Youth & Family Institute. We are an organization committed to one thing, vibrant faith formation. We would argue that spiritual development is a core part of being human. Like physical, emotional, or cognitive development, spiritual development takes place only if it is nurtured and cultivated. This requires wisdom, effective practices, commitment, and energy. Because spiritual development is a core part of being human, we consider our work a sacred trust and feel that congregations and homes share that same sacred trust. We are all called by God to "nurture the spark" that can glow brightly in ourselves and our young people.

We have all looked into the eyes of a child, a youth, or an adult where the spirit has been smothered, the spark snuffed out, and the light gone dim. In place of that vibrant faith resides a deep, dark black hole that often is filled with anger, suspicion, hurt, doubt, and fear. This should never happen to anyone.

And we have all looked into the eyes of a child, a youth, or an adult where their spirit has been tended and their faith explored. These eyes show curiosity, wisdom, energy, trust, and joy. God wills for all human eyes to reveal such a vibrant faith. It is to this end that David Anderson has written and toward which we work at The Youth & Family Institute.

Dr. Paul G. Hill
Executive Director

Introduction

From the Great Omission to Vibrant Faith

The Christian church is in a time of major transition. It is both a time filled with immense opportunity and a time of deep challenge, especially in the church of the northern hemisphere and particularly for the church in the United States. That church is pursuing a clear identity and purpose in and for the twenty-first century. This book contributes to this period of identity formation and purposeful focus for the life of the church in the American context.

Christian Faith in the Home

The observations and recommendations for the church made here center on one significant component in human development and, therefore, to the life of the Christian faith: the recognition of the role of the home as a critical player in the lives of individuals and communities. One need not idealize or worship the family or the larger sense of home to acknowledge that the primary life experiences and relationships that begin very early in life are formative. And yet, for many Christian leaders, the home has largely been ignored as a significant—even God-given—tool for formation of the spiritual life. This book addresses the need to elevate the role of the home and offers suggestions for recovering the life of the home as an essential ingredient to the ministry of congregations and the larger church.

It is respectfully acknowledged that giving attention to the home is not a new cause or strategy in the church. In recent generations the role of the home has, in fact, been lifted up by various groups in numerous ways. However, those voices and that movement often have failed to get traction in the life of the church. Lifting up a vision that values the role of the home and offering some resources to help families of various shapes and sizes has not been enough to establish the home as a critical player in the life of the church. Something more is needed to go from idea to reality. That something more, addressed in this book and in the larger Vibrant Faith series, combines a number of elements.

The Home in the Bible and Christian History
First, church leaders—clergy and lay, including paid staff and elected and appointed servants—can focus on the biblical and historical precedence for the role of the home. It is not enough for our congregations to give the appearance of being "family friendly" by welcoming people into the life of the congregation. The goal is to equip homes through the life of the congregation so that when people return home, they have the encouragement, faith resources, and vision to be the people of God in and through their own homes. In this way the home reclaims its rightful place as an expression of the church. Attention to the importance of the home in Scripture, the history of the church, and even modern research helps us avoid a fad that is temporary, for example, a new twist to being the church that somehow emulates a perceived life of the American family from the 1950s.

Reclaiming Language
Next, congregational leaders need to be strengthened not only with the conviction that reclaiming the role of the home is warranted but with

a particular language that communicates and serves the work of the church (what this book and series refers to as the Vibrant Faith Frame), with awareness of imminent challenges, and with leadership strategies that have shown themselves to work in real-life congregational settings and homes. *From the Great Omission to Vibrant Faith* does just that. The other two volumes in the Vibrant Faith series go into more detail to offer concrete examples, resources, and strategies to make the Vibrant Faith Frame come alive in the various ministry areas in the congregation (volume 2) and in the life of the home (volume 3).

> Giving attention to the home is not a new cause or strategy in the church.

Defining the Great Omission

From the Great Omission to Vibrant Faith equips congregational leaders with a vision, biblical and historical references, language, insights, strategies, concrete examples from homes and congregations, and approaches to leadership that will help congregations value, equip, and renew the life of the home as a means to value, equip, and renew the life of the congregation. Chapter 1 names the neglect of the role of home as the Great Omission in the life of the twentieth-century (and now the twenty-first-century) church in America. It faces the sensitive issue of defining family in a way that is more inclusive and more biblical than the modern, twentieth-century stereotype of family.

Home and family as understood here includes a cross+generational component, a bringing together of multiple generations to pass on faith, values, and character formation. "Cross+generational" is a term used in the language of the Vibrant Faith Frame instead of "inter-generational" to emphasize that for the Christian community, the cross of Christ binds the generations together in faith-shaping ways. The chapter offers examples of what the church in the home and the church in the congregation can look like as a cross+generational community when the Great Omission is averted and the life of the home is celebrated as a contributor to Christian faith formation.

Confronting the Great Omission

Chapter 2 presents the Vibrant Faith Frame as a means to confront the Great Omission. It provides the language that helps church leaders in congregations and homes name, claim, and value how God is at work in our lives and communities. The Vibrant Faith Frame can be labeled numerically as the 6-5-4-3. It begins with the Six Locations of Ministry that observe that the mission of the church is both personal and local as well as communal and global. Then the Five Principles describe the dynamics of faith formation in the church. The principles point out that faith formation is relational, experiential, and honors the home as church too, where Christ is present in faith. The means to live this faith daily in the world is described through the Four Keys, foundational faith practices that unassumingly weave into the fabric of everyday life. The goal of all this is the "AAA" Christian, the disciple of Christ who is authentic, available, and affirming. What makes this material more than theory or tenuous possibility is the numerous examples that come from the actual accounts of congregations using the Vibrant Faith Frame.

Wrestling with the Great Omission

Chapter 3 revisits the theme of the Great Omission, pointing out how the church has in some ways been held captive by it and offering biblical commentary to negate those who think Jesus did not care about the family. The chapter gives literary and historic examples of the de-emphasis on the life of the home—especially the role of parents—and toward a dependence on "experts" to raise our children for church and society. The chapter presupposes that recognizing the thorny presence of the Great Omission is the best way for congregational leaders to move beyond its limitation on effective congregational ministry.

Beyond the Great Omission

The remaining chapters give specific suggestions to congregational leaders as they adopt the Vibrant Faith Frame for the discipleship and evangelism of the church. In chapter 4, leaders are cautioned not to blame parents for their shortcomings as spiritual mentors in the home. For decades parents and other caregivers of children and youth have not been honored for their vital roles. Now they need to be supported and given the tools to nurture faith, values, and character formation.

Chapter 5 advocates for a specific model of congregational leadership that fosters transformational change. This means more than good organizational skills and development. It means offering spiritual care by the leaders—especially but not exclusively the pastor—and it means offering spiritual care to those who are in leadership roles themselves.

Chapter 6 offers and explains four tips for leaders committed to the Vibrant Faith Frame: get fluent with the language, be patient, help people develop new habits, and acknowledge that doubt is a part of biblical faith. The final chapter endorses the importance of doing congregational research, the kind of relational checking in with people that finds out how the Vibrant Faith Frame is impacting lives and what more can be done to help individuals and households live a vibrant faith that is authentic, available, and affirming.

A Vibrant Faith

For the sake of transformational change in the lives of Christians and to strengthen the mission and ministry of the church, this volume encourages leaders to pursue their own authentic, available, and affirming faith. This needs to be pursued in the spirit of the words of Paul in Philippians, "Work out your own salvation with fear and trembling; for it is God who is at work in you, enabling you both to will and to work for his good pleasure" (2:12b-13). Nothing of value happens to the people of God without the word of God, the Spirit of God, the will of God as foundational to it all. As leaders commit to their faith formation with this focus on the will and work of God, their own leadership will have integrity as they guide and mentor with patience and persistence. They need to be patient with people because habits and thought processes tend to put new wine into old wine skins. It takes time to construct new wineskins that will be able to hold onto the new wine of the Vibrant Faith Frame. It is not that the ideas, practices, and strategies behind the Vibrant Faith Frame is actually new, however. It just appears new to recent generations of churchgoers. Leaders need to be persistent, because without the constant awareness and utilization of the Vibrant Faith Frame, congregations and homes cannot gain familiarity and fluency with the language and Christian practices that will guide the faith lives of individuals, homes, and congregations.

The Great Omission

One Modest but Indispensable Claim

From the Great Omission to Vibrant Faith makes one modest claim, simply and directly. Faith is formed by the power of the Holy Spirit through personal, trusted relationships—often in our own homes. It is modest not only because all claims about faith formation depend upon a gracious, merciful, judging, discerning, just, wise, and loving God but because there are many worthwhile contributions to congregational renewal and leadership. This is but one. This book also offers one rather obvious ingredient to congregational renewal, one obvious and foundational ingredient to reviving the church that has been most always ignored in recent decades: the home. Where Christ is present in faith, the home is church too. Because the home is a place where God's people dwell and prepare to serve in the larger world, it is a place worthy of the attention and support of local congregations as part of the renewal of the life of the larger church.

This omitted principle may seem rather unexceptional. But it represents a factor in congregational life that has immense impact on most everything else in the life of the church. The homes of those affiliated with a local congregation represent the church life outside the walls of the congregation. The public assembly of Christians in a local congregation lives in a powerful and meaningful relationship with those who gather regularly in homes and through homes to the larger community, culture, and world. The church that gathers in the congregation partners with the church that gathers and lives in homes, and this dynamic impacts worship, Christian education, youth ministry, fellowship, service to others, and a more comprehensive understanding of discipleship, evangelism, and stewardship. Those who arrive to the public gathering of the congregation arrive from daily lives of faith lived, celebrated, and tested in real time in real relationships in the midst of real life-and-death issues, the kind that happen in and through the life of the home.

A Painful Reality

A group of active members in a once-thriving congregation gathered for a presentation on the vital partnership between the ministry of the congregation and the ministry of the home. The people heard that the Silent (Booster) Generation, those born generally between 1924 and 1944, represented the most churched generation in U.S. history. The audience also heard that the Silent Generation gave birth to the Baby Boom Generation, what became the least churched generation in U.S. history. Baby Boomers begat the next generation, an even less-churched generation. This downward trend continues through subsequent generations.

The pain on the faces of those gathered was evident. A significant reason for the problem was dawning on them: Sunday school, confirmation class, and youth programs were never enough to engage children and youth in the life of the Christian faith and the church. A sense of guilt came over a number of the adults. They had driven their children to congregational activities, but the faith life often was not modeled in their own homes. Many of their grown children no longer were part of the church. One gentleman said with resignation, "But we did what we were told to do, 'Get them to church.'"

Recent generations have been doing what church leaders have requested of them: "Get your kids to us, and we will raise them for you in the Christian faith." The problem is that it does not always work. That strategy and that understanding of what it means to be the church was incomplete.

> **But we did what we were told to do, 'Get them to church.'**

Identifying the Great Omission

At the end of the Gospel of Matthew, Jesus gives the church what has been called the Great Commission: "Go therefore and make disciples of all nations, baptizing them in the name of the Father and of the Son and of the Holy Spirit, and teaching them to obey everything that I have commanded you. And remember, I am with you always, to the end of the age" (Matthew 28:19-20). These final verses in Matthew remind the church of the fundamental task of making disciples. The reclaiming of that fundamental task (as opposed to the congregational task of making members) is at the heart of today's church renewal.

However, the church's ongoing reformation and renewal cannot be effective as long as the church pursues the Great Commission while at the same time committing the Great Omission, the neglect of the role of the home in making disciples. The omission of the home as a vital partner with the public congregational life has hampered attempts to revive the outreach focus of the church in recent decades. Factoring in the role of the home is not the only important ingredient to congregational renewal; it is simply the one consistently overlooked by teachers, authors, and practitioners of congregational renewal proposals. The examples are numerous in the current literature. Many wonderful efforts in diverse circles have fostered congregational renewal. But this one glaring omission remains. Without rejecting these other efforts, we must lift up what often is missing in the attempt to renew our congregations and to pass on the Christian faith to a variety of generations and communities: the role of the home.

The strong—even provocative—language of the Great Omission and the description of it in this book do not suggest that all church leaders and congregations have neglected the role of the home. But enough leaders and congregations have neglected the role of the home that negative consequences for homes and congregations across the church are evident. To put it simply, the Great Omission is hindering the renewal of the church. The imagery of the Great Omission also conveys that even in those congregations that specifically value the role of the home, practice often lags behind theory. The congregations may assume or even speak of the importance of family and home life, but these same congregations often fail to implement practices that strengthen the faith life of the home. This is part of what is referred to as the Great Omission.

A Contribution to Church Renewal

A wonderful focus for the renewal of the church is right under our noses, the homes of people who worship, study, serve, and play in our own congregational settings. These homes provide the immediate and essential context for faith, moral, and character formation from the earliest stages of life until our dying breath. The church must understand how relatives and friends are already servants of the church evangelizing the world and fostering faith formation in daily life contexts. So a fundamental goal of this book and the larger Vibrant Faith series is to reinstate the role of the home to its rightful place as a God-given tool for the ministry of Jesus Christ. In other words, it is time to recover from the Great Omission of neglecting the home as a vital partner in the work of the church.

Pastor Tim Glenham from Morning Star Lutheran Church in Matthews, North Carolina, is one of those pastors in one of those congregations that has moved from the Great Omission to a focus on the Christian faith in the home. Each month he has a different council member tell a story of how God is at work in her or his daily life, especially in and through the home. He has the council member tell the story and then write it up so that it can be a word of encouragement and faith to others. Although council members routinely do this activity and communicate their stories with the larger congregation, other members in the congregation are invited to do so as well. After some months of reading the faith stories of council members, one dad volunteered his own story. What follows is his own account.

Recently I started a new ritual I learned from church.

My daughter Samantha is three. Every night it's: "Daddy will you tuck me in"? "Of course" is always my answer (and with joy). But this night would be different. After I covered Sam up, rubbed her back and stroked her hair like I normally do, this night I leaned over and made the sign of the cross on her forehead. Then I whispered in her ear, "God made you special and I Love You." Then off I went to finish my nightly routines.

That was two months ago, and it continues to this day. I go into Sam's room and I whisper in her ear: "God made you special and I love you." That is a rich blessing. But the true blessing of that ritual came back to me in a surprising, heart warming way.

A few weeks ago, after a longer than normal weekend being away with our church youth group, I didn't arise to see Sam off to school on Monday as I do every morning. So on that Monday, at 6:45 in the morning, I hear the sound of little feet coming into my bedroom. With no light on, Sam gently lifted the covers and pulled them up to my neck. As I rolled over to look at her smiling face, she quietly took her finger and made the sign of the cross on my forehead and whispered in my ear: "God made you special and I Love You." Then just as quietly as she entered, she tiptoed out of the room and off for school.

When we give, we receive; and sometimes in some of the most surprising, least expected, heartfelt, and wonderful ways. By passing on faith to Sam, she passed it back to me, thus completing that circle. I can't wait to discover other ways, in other new areas, to plant the seed and let it grow.

The story may appear to be from one of those ideal home settings where everything seems to go right. However, this story comes from a man who has experienced his ups and downs in life, including his family life. After a divorce and remarriage, he is learning from the challenges and struggles of life. What makes his story even more powerful and helpful is that it comes from one who in many ways characterizes the lives of so many others.

Pastor Glenham stated that when this father told his story, he became filled with emotion, his eyes became moist, and he had to pause and regroup in order to finish the story. The point is that council members, dads, people who have experienced the challenges of family life, and a lot of other folk are touched deeply by God's presence in relationships, especially those in our own homes.

The Extended Home

Nurturing the Christian faith in the home is not simply about stories of families with small children. It follows the whole gamut of life experiences with friends and family members. In May 2008 Merv, a husband, father, and grandfather, was dying of acute leukemia at age eighty-eight. As the family would soon learn, he was within forty-eight hours of his own death. On his last Sunday night, he was surrounded by young adult grandchildren, two daughters, a son-in-law, and his wife of more than sixty years.

That day one of his grandsons had asked what he liked to eat, and Merv said, "Cream." "What kind of cream, Grandpa?" came the reply. "Banana cream," murmured Merv. Several of the family members took off and picked up a couple of pies at a local restaurant, including Grandpa's favorite. That evening the family sat down with Grandpa for dinner. One of the granddaughters present suggested that the meal begin with dessert in honor of Grandpa. It was a memorable meal. Following the feast of banana cream pie, meat, potatoes, and more, the three-generational family sat down in the living room to read Matthew 11:28-30 (one of Grandpa's favorite Bible verses and a very fitting passage for a number of reasons that night), pray, sing hymns, and have holy communion. His wife asked, "Honey, are you looking forward to heaven?" "Yes," was the answer. She continued, "Are you ready to die?" "Not yet," was the strong response. The final action was to gather around a grandfather, father, and husband, lay loving hands on his shoulders, and bless him as he approached his final days.

That night three generations of loved ones experienced the power of the Christian faith to support and encourage a dying husband, father, and grandfather. The evening was filled with foundational faith practices of caring conversations, devotions, service, and rituals and traditions (explored in chapter 2 as the Four Keys). Framed with tears, love, laughter, and honest responses, three generations of the church were blessed as together they touched the mystery of life and death with faith, hope, and love. It was the kind of evening—the kind of worship—that needed to take place at the home of Grandma and Grandpa. It was also the kind of evening that would impact them all for a lifetime, including special memories forever present around banana cream pie.

Something Has Gotten in the Way

Something has gotten in the way of these stories becoming better known in the life of the church. The stories are there, and the impact on faith formation is happening. That's the good news. Unfortunately, something has interfered with our attention to the important dynamic of the home in Christian discipleship: the Great Omission of the church. The church is not as aware as it could be to the life- and faith-shaping experiences that can—and sometimes still do—happen in the context of the life of the home.

Often the Great Omission of the church is rather subtle. What follows is one example from a fine book on congregational staff team ministry. The author writes in a chapter entitled "The Empowering Team":

> People care about how the leaders get along and function together. Their own families and work environments are full of dysfunctional relationships and conflict. People want to know if the church leaders can learn to work together, and if they can, their model will have a powerful influence

throughout the church and even the town or city at large. It is that powerful and influential.[1]

It is interesting how easy it is to say or write about "dysfunctional" families, as though it were the norm. On the one hand, there are those like Stephanie Coontz[2] who would argue that it has become all too easy to consider today's families dysfunctional or in some other sense unhealthy. As the argument goes, there is a memory of more pristine families from the past that were not as healthy or wholesome as we may think. Today's families, therefore, may not be as unhealthy, especially if they are not compared to a mythological past that never existed. In other words, today's families get unfair criticism, particularly families that are not like ours (our own families tend to be credited as the more healthy and functional families!). On the other hand, of course, dysfunctional families are the norm. Dysfunction is a way of life for broken, sinful creatures. So it is true that you could probably find quite a bit of dysfunction on a championship athletic team, or in an American president's cabinet, or in a corporate board, or in a congregation. So what's new?

Missed in such a comment about dysfunctional life is that God can work in and through dysfunction just as Jesus worked through prejudice, rejection, torture, and death, and just like God was at work in the home of the dad from Morning Star and the home of Merv and his family. The grace and mercy of God is like that.

Also missing is that when the author goes on to describe the positive impact of functioning well as a team, he associates it with its impact on the congregation and town or city but not the family! The author reflects a contemporary assumption that it is just too much to imagine today's families as healthy. What a missed opportunity to help congregational leaders perceive their positive influence on family life, one of God's great influences on individuals and communities.

Subtle and not-so-subtle rebukes and silence regarding the home is the norm for church leadership literature. In your congregation's library or a staff member's own bookshelves you will find these leadership books on congregational renewal. One will not find the home talked about or one will find it talked about in pejorative ways (most often the former). There is very little evidence of the vital partnership between home and congregation that is part of the historic church evidenced in the New Testament. The home will not be lifted up as a means for the Holy Spirit to enliven the church throughout the ages. The home as a way of being the church has been overlooked by the church in America through at least the later half of the twentieth century and beyond.

> " Family life is not easy, perfect, or the sole answer. "

Recovering from the Great Omission as the Third Way

To a significant degree, what has been lost in the church is the value of family itself. The Christian community has not sufficiently defined or promoted a viable life of faith for home and family. With all the cultural, political, and religious talk about "family values," this observation might seem a bit odd. However, there is a big difference between the rhetoric of family values and the actual practice of valuing families as a God-given source of faith formation.

As some talk of family values, others react negatively to it as a politicized concept. The negative reaction tends to undervalue the gift of daily life relationships in and through the home. Between these two cultural poles is a third way, a way that does not limit the life of the family to political sound bites and does not throw out the value of family life with the bath water of family values. The third way is to recapture the role of the home in passing on faith, values, and character formation.

Defining Family

Let the reader beware. The vision for church renewal for a vibrant faith proposed here does not suggest that family life is easy, perfect, or the sole answer. The role of the family has been ignored recently in part because of an implicit embarrassment regarding its failings, sometimes associated with the families of church leaders themselves.

The term "family" is difficult to use in congregations or to define within our larger society. The way it will be understood here is not the 1950s version of *Father Knows Best*, the *Donna Reed Show*, or *Leave It to Beaver*, where family life ends up neat and tidy at the end of each episode. This is not a "family values" agenda that sees the home as offering some kind of ideal existence that protects children from the harsh realities of life and the immorality of the surrounding culture. Family life can be raw as well as comforting; it can be brutal as well as safe; it can be sad and painful as well as delightful and playful. Family life offers all the above, a world of real feelings, experiences, and struggles that need the grace of God to bless and to heal. Family life also offers a network of relationships that connects it to the world beyond the walls of the home and the congregation to a larger environment of relationships, of needs, of learning, of meaning, and of hope, the larger world to which the Christian community is called.

In this book the word "home" is used often as a synonym for "family." In our society and especially in the church, the term "family" by itself and without clarification has become divisive and therefore unhelpful, excluding people who do not fit a narrow understanding of family life. In fact, there is no biblical term for *family* as we typically understand the term in our modern times in America. Today it often implies a two-generational package with parents and children living in the same dwelling. The biblical understanding of home or family is much larger and more inclusive (more cross+generational). For example, Genesis 17:27 notes that the men of Abraham's house included not only his son Ishmael (Ishmael was thirteen at the time, and Isaac was not yet born) but also Abraham's "slaves born in the house and those bought with money from a foreigner." Even in the New Testament times, family included husbands and wives, parents and children, master and slaves, as well as extended family members like in-laws (see Colossians 3:18-24, 1 Timothy 5:3-8).

The idea of family presented here includes others besides parents and children. It elevates those who function in the role of family life. Family can be those people in one's life who provide the kind of support, care, and guidance over time that serves the function of siblings, uncles, aunts, grandparents, or parents. The United States now has a forty-fourth president whose own biography embodies this: Barack Obama was raised for years by his maternal grandparents.

The term "over time" is important. The kind of support, care, and guidance of which we speak most often cannot take place without the investment of real time. A good example is the process of learning a language. Those who teach you how to speak your native language do so over time, a long time, and they include your family members.

Whether the term is "family" or "home," in the Christian context the words connote a communal context of life out of which one moves to enter into the larger world as a child of God and to which one routinely returns to be nourished, strengthened, sheltered, and guided as a child of God. Through this intimate environment of home, of family, one lives out her or his calling in God's creation. Jesus certainly alludes to this understanding of family when he said, "'Here are my mother and my brothers! Whoever does the will of God is my brother and sister and mother'" (Mark 3:34b-35). We hear that kind of care, guidance, and instruction in Deuteronomy 6: "Recite [these words] to your children and talk about them when you are at home and when you are away, when you lie down and when you rise. Bind them as a sign on your hand, fix them as an emblem on your forehead, and write them on the doorposts of your house and on your gates" (6:7-9). In this seminal text, home life or family life (notice parents are not mentioned by name at all in this text) passes on the faith and the life of faith through words spoken, words written, words expressed and lived in daily life experiences away from home and in the home.

A person can enjoy a rich family life while living alone in one's home or with others who are not kin by marriage, birth, or adoption. Although the term "family" will necessarily be used at times in this book, the term home will often be used to avoid a more exclusive understanding of family that tends to creep into one's mind no matter what a speaker or author intends. Whether discussing one's home or one's family, the point is that this intimate community in one's life shapes faith, values, and character development for a lifetime. And the most complete experience of this home or family includes a multitude of generations interacting together. In its most helpful, life-shaping, and faith-forming dimensions, it is a cross+generational experience.

Reclaiming the Larger Sense of Family in Congregations

Once the cross+generational experience of family life is embraced by a congregation, it begins to impact both the interactions within the congregation as well as one's pursuit of family life experiences in daily life. Julie Luttinen Miller (at the time single and Julie Luttinen) gives a wonderful example of this as a youth and family director whose congregation was embracing and applying the Vibrant Faith Frame (see chapter 2 for a full description of the Vibrant Faith Frame). The congregation had just completed the TYFI preaching and teaching series based on the book I authored with Paul Hill, *Frogs without Legs Can't Hear: Nurturing Disciples in Home and Congregation*. Julie Miller volunteered an evaluation of the impact of the preaching and teaching series in the congregation. Notice how she expands the understanding of family in both the congregational and domestic settings. She writes,

> We have a woman in our congregation who lost her husband at the beginning of Lent. Last week she made the connection with another single woman in the congregation who is desperately looking for a "faith family" as well. We were in the book study discussing "Frogs" [the book Frogs without Legs Can't Hear] and during Caring Conversation they made the connection. They are now meeting regularly to practice the Four Keys [See pp. 49–52 for an explanation of the Four Keys.].

> Our young adults in the congregation (there are only five of us, including me) mostly live alone or with a roommate. We've decided to be each other's "household" and have started to gather to share a meal and practice the Four Keys together as a "family."

For me the most powerful evidence of the program's effec-
tiveness lies in the quiet moments I observe before or after ser-
vices. I have witnessed countless acts of "faith catching" [see
the Five Principles in chapter 2 and especially principle 4: faith
is caught more than it is taught] between adults and youth in
our congregation. They don't even seem to know what's hap-
pening! They just sit and talk. A 50s-plus member high-fives
an eighth-grade boy after he finds out he aced his math test.
A Senior High girl who attends church by herself is invited
to lunch with another family from the church after worship.
Another young girl who hasn't been around for awhile is wel-
comed back with a smile and a hug by a woman who looks
forward to sitting and visiting with her during coffee hour.

I'm not sure you would count any of this as "evidence" of
getting it, but I do. It is amazing to watch the Holy Spirit at
work in this congregation right now.

This youth and family director observed and described what we at
TYFI mean by family and the life of the home to nurture the Christian faith. Women looking for a sense of community and support,
young adult peers looking for a sense of family or "household," adults
in a congregation recognizing the importance of reaching out to
youth with whom they, as adults, have a real impact. These examples
clearly expand our understanding of family while not ignoring that
parents with children in the home fit this understanding as well.

Beyond the Great Omission to the Great Commission

As the congregation described above reclaimed the larger sense of
family, it began to overcome the Great Omission and move forward
to strengthen its work of the Great Commission. That represents the
desired outcome of the Vibrant Faith Frame, the church addressing
the Great Commission, addressing the critical task of making and
nurturing disciples without committing the Great Omission.

The personal, trusted relationships that we rely on over time and that are referred to here as "family," "household," or "home" provide an ingredient to discipleship that simply cannot be ignored any longer. The family might look like a mom and (or) a dad with one or more children. It might look very different from that. People function as family in many ways, whether or not they are connected to one another by birth, marriage, or adoption. It might be a family without children or one that has three or more generations bonded together. The family may live under one roof or relate to one another through means other than a common address. The families to which the Vibrant Faith Frame refers include a multitude of intimate and sustaining communities. It could include a support group, prayer partners, friends, coworkers, and neighbors. Reclaiming this larger sense of family will help individuals and congregations move beyond the Great Omission and on to the Great Commission.

2

THE VIBRANT FAITH FRAME

The Vibrant Faith Frame establishes an understanding of the essential work of the church, strategic practices to be engaged by the church, and a description of the outcome of the work of the church. The Vibrant Faith Frame is the outgrowth of the work of The Youth & Family Institute. TYFI serves the church as a Christian organization dedicated to help strengthen congregations, homes, and individuals by equipping them to live a vibrant faith in Jesus Christ that is authentic, available, and affirming. The Vibrant Faith Frame has emerged over years of research on faith formation, including biblical, theological, and congregational study and actual work with congregations across the United States and occasionally beyond the United States in Canada, Australia, Norway, and Sweden. This ministry framework has come to be known through a numerical sequence that identifies the major elements of the Vibrant Faith Frame: 6-5-4-3. The numbers refer to the Six Locations of Ministry, the Five Principles of a vibrant church, and the foundational faith practices called the Four Keys, all of which culminate in a AAA Christian Disciple.

After a conference near Omaha, Nebraska, from TYFI on what is now referred to as the Vibrant Faith Frame, a seasoned pastor I knew when I was a relatively new pastor in Nebraska came up to me and said, "Ya know, I have been thinking this way for seventeen years. You just gave me the language to express it. Thanks." The language we use to describe the Christian life and faith assumes a vision of the church and its ministry. Although today's church is making important strides, too often the language of the church remains indebted to a vision of the church that looks and sounds like a public institution that thinks, speaks, and operates in terms of constitutions, boards, committees, budgets, organization, buildings, ideas, and membership. The church must endorse and use more regularly a language and a vision that speaks also about relationships, mission, discerning, following, prayer and other faith practices, risk, the cross, and discipleship.

The glossary of terms provided by the Vibrant Faith Frame supports a vision of the church that is more relational in nature—more in relationship to a living and gracious God and more in relationship to the presence of God in other people. The language of the Vibrant Faith Frame presents a form of DNA for the church, that is, the life-giving building blocks for being the body of Christ in the world. The glossary of terms does not present one specific model for being the church. Thinking in terms of models would be too specific and limiting for a church that exists in countless different mission fields and contexts. I have on occasion presented the Vibrant Faith Frame only to have someone try to dismiss the presentation, "It's different here in (name your own community)." The Vibrant Faith DNA is not about surface appearances like a tattoo or a one-size-fits-all approach to healthy congregations. It simply suggests basic stuff for the life of the church that goes deep into the marrow of its very being. It can morph into many different shapes, sizes, and experiences, but this DNA of the church remains.

The terms present in the Vibrant Faith Frame are helpful to the extent that they enable a process of giving attention and imagination to the God-reality of our lives. The process goes like this:

- Name it
- Claim it
- Value it
- Reinforce it
- Recommit to it
- Name it again

The Frame gives language to name how God is present in our lives (for example, "Faith is formed by the power of the Holy Spirit through personal trusted relationships."). Once we can name it, we can claim it as God's work in our own lives, not just a theory or conjecture but as our own experience (for example, the Four Keys). Once we have done that, we are well on our way to valuing this divine narrative of being claimed by the work and will of God for good, for healing, for salvation, for grace and mercy, and for peace. Once we have named, claimed, and valued God's work in our lives, we are at the same time reinforcing the value of God's work in our lives and in our world.

Through this process and sequence, the God-reality looms as a larger part of who we are, of our identity. In the words of the apostle Paul, "It is no longer I who live, but Christ who lives in me" (Galatians 2:20). The final step in this process of embracing the divine narrative of our lives is to recommit to the cycle of naming, claiming, valuing, and reinforcing our awareness of the God-reality, the life more attuned and responsive to the word and will of God in our lives. It is the life measured in terms of a worldview shaped by language like grace, mercy, and peace.

When the pastor said he has been thinking this way for seventeen years but without the clarity of language (and therefore vision), he was in essence stating that he now has the glossary to identify and respond more clearly to the God-reality of life. That happens with more clarity and regularity as he—and we—name, claim, value, reinforce, and recommit to the life marked by Christ through language like the Vibrant Faith Frame.

THE VIBRANT FAITH FRAME GLOSSARY OF TERMS

6 SIX LOCATIONS of ministry

- Children and youth
- Homes
- Congregations
- Community
- Culture
- Creation

5 FIVE PRINCIPLES of a vibrant church

- Faith is formed by the power of the Holy Spirit through personal trusted relationships—often in our own homes.
- The church is a living partnership between the ministry of the congregation and ministry of the home.
- Where Christ is present in faith, the home is church, too.
- Faith is caught more than it is taught.
- If we want Christian children and youth, we need Christian adults.

4 FOUR KEYS for practicing faith

- Caring Conversations
- Devotions
- Service
- Rituals and Traditions

3 THREE CHARACTERISTICS of Christian disciples

- Authentic
- Available
- Affirming

This chapter presents concepts and language developed in the rest of the book. For a more detailed analysis of the concepts that follow, one can read *Frogs without Legs Can't Hear: Nurturing Disciples in Home and Congregation* by David W. Anderson and Paul Hill (Minneapolis: Augsburg Fortress, 2003), which offers a detailed analysis of the Five Principles, Four Keys, and AAA Christian Disciple. For a much closer look at the Six Locations of Ministry, one can turn to *Passing on the Faith* by Merton Strommen and Richard Hardel (both authors are former executive directors of TYFI).

Six Locations of Ministry

The value of the Six Locations of Ministry is that it identifies the context for Christian ministry and reminds the church that the work of the kingdom of God impacts individuals, homes, congregations, community, culture, and creation. It also acknowledges that the ministry of the church is directly impacted by the contributions and needs of individuals, homes, congregations, community, culture, and creation. The Six Locations of Ministry reclaims what the church at times seems to forget, especially in an individualized American culture (that "pick-yourself-up-by-your-own-bootstrap" mentality also referenced as "rugged individualism" and the "frontier spirit"). Specifically, the church forgets that Christianity involves more than one's personal (read "private") relationship with Jesus. The God of the church is the God who redeems not only individual lives but all of creation (Romans 8:19-23, see also Psalm 104 and 148). The Christian church worships the God of creation who loves all that God creates (John 3:16) and promises to redeem all things with a new heaven and a new earth (Revelation 21:1). The church lives in praise and thanksgiving for all that God restores and reconciles in Christ (2 Corinthians 5:17-19). To be the church and pass on faith in Christ requires attention to all that God does and all that God calls Christians to be in the world. This may be well expressed in John 3:8: the Spirit of God blows wherever it wills.

Children and youth: They are recognized and equipped as disciples of Jesus Christ, accomplishing important ministry and receiving care for their physical, emotional, cognitive, relational, and spiritual development throughout all of life. In the eyes of the church, every person no matter their age is a child of God worthy of attention and care. Placing children and youth in the center of the schemata is a way to state that children and youth are central to the life of the church. They are the litmus test of the health of the church. As the Maasai warriors greet one another asking, "How are the children," so too the people of the body of Christ can ask the same questions. In either case, the question is, "How is the wellbeing of our community?"

The tendency in the church is to put children and youth off on the periphery in their own space, meeting at their own times and led by their own children and youth leaders. A pastor from Australia confirmed this tendency when he told the story of asking his twenty-four-year-old daughter why she was no longer part of the church after being so involved in the youth group. She responded, "You're right Dad, I was active in the youth group. I was never active in the church."

Homes: Individuals living in close connection to one another in family-type relationships that offer foundational care for people of all ages. While this means a rich variety of relationships, parents deserve particular attention for the support and honor due their vital service to children and the larger society. Homes of diverse types, including those without children, represent the larger understanding of family life cared for by the love of God and the work of the body of Christ. The term "home" represents much more than an address. Home represents the larger network of personal relationships that connects people to one another in more intimate and daily settings like one's dwelling, one's workplace, and one's community. The life of the home pays attention to and thus serves this larger network of relationships experienced in daily life. When the Christian faith is present in these family-type relationships, the home represents the domestic expression of the church.

Congregations: These local expressions of the church bring people together to be given new life through the means of grace in Christ and also send people back out to homes, communities, and the world to learn where and how to serve, to bless, and to give praise to God in daily life. Congregations represent the larger network of relationships that connect Christians to larger church structures and the ministries those structures represent.

Community: In this immediate social, economic, political, educational, and religious environment, Christians have their most direct experience of faith made active in love that serves neighbor and creation. It is also from the community that Christians themselves are cared for and equipped for service to others through education and community services that equip as well as protect people's lives.

Culture: Christians experience God's presence, learning from people from a variety of cultures while being part of God's transformational work within culture. It is culture that gives the languages people speak. That language conveys meaning and interprets experiences that are both affirmed and challenged by the church.

Creation: Christians live as stewards of God's handiwork in creation, recognizing, receiving, celebrating, and serving all that God creates, redeems, and sustains.

The 5-4-3

While the Six Locations of Ministry identify the context for Christian ministry that imagines and responds to all that God has created and redeemed in Christ, the 5-4-3 presents the breakthrough contributions that address the Great Omission and offer the unique heart of Christian ministry presented by the Vibrant Faith Frame.

The First and Pivotal Principle: Faith is formed by the power of the Holy Spirit through personal, trusted relationships—often in our own homes

For congregational leaders to grasp the life of faith beyond congregational activities like Sunday school and worship, it works best to have them relate to their own faith stories, their own experiences. When TYFI works with a congregational staff to introduce the Vibrant Faith Frame, a standard exercise is to have them as a group name a person or event that has influenced their life of faith. Below are the answers from the last three congregational staff that have done this exercise prior to the writing of this book:

Congregation A

Who or What Has Influenced Your Life of Faith?

Grandmother

Mother

Pastor's wife

Girlfriend who became wife

Sunday school teacher

Preschool director (adult mentor to preschool staff member)

Congregation B

Who or What Has Influenced Your Life of Faith?

Grandma

Mother

Parish worker

Daughter

Mom and dad

Mom and dad

Campus Crusade for Christ

Grandma

Mom and dad

Pastor

Confirmation class

Congregation C

Who or What Has Influenced Your Life of Faith?

Grandmother

Ingvar, a boring Sunday school teacher

Oprah Winfrey

Elaine, a dear friend

Grandmother

Dad

Mother

Parents

Mike, an older gentleman from the congregation

Dad

Mother

These lists are nothing new, although after twenty years of doing this exercise with scores of congregations, Oprah Winfrey was a first. The other answers, however, tend to confirm the rule of the influence of personal, trusted relationships. Parents and grandparents are the norm in such lists. Spouses and children are not unusual. Confirmation class is clearly an exception but is mentioned on occasion. Often when an educational program or congregational leader like a pastor or Sunday school teacher is mentioned, behind that answer is a personal, trusted relationship, like Ingvar, the boring Sunday school teacher, who in spite of his teaching methods or delivery left a lasting impression on at least one student. This is also true for the pastor whose sermons were not necessarily memorable but who cared about the individual or the individual's family.

Surprising about these lists is that they so clearly confirm the first of the Five Principles (faith formed through personal, trusted relationships), even though the respondents are congregational staff. If anyone would identify and support programs (Sunday school, confirmation class, youth groups, and so on) and leaders from the institutional church (pastors, youth workers, and Sunday school teachers, and so on), we would assume it would be the people who have been inspired to develop these programs and become those leaders. The point is all the more graphic because even our congregational staff acknowledge that the influence on their own faith goes back to personal, trusted relationships, often relationships experienced early in life and connected to the home as a child. This is not intended to indicate an either/or between personal, trusted relationships and congregational programs. It does indicate, however, that personal, trusted relationships loom large for the faith formation of people, including people who promote congregational programs.

Unless their own testimony and their own experiences are presented to them, the knee-jerk response on how to influence a person's faith tends to go straight to the congregation's programmatic life, especially Christian education, youth ministry, and worship. The prevailing assumption is that if you want to do the work of the kingdom of God, the only option is to build bigger buildings, offer more programs, and stand in front of the masses and inspire! How did poor,

boring Ingvar ever make the cut? If one does not start from the premise that public institutions can go it alone, and if one starts from one's
own experience instead of congregational leadership theories and
assumptions, one might just discover in the stories and experiences
within the Christian community the data that identify what actually
influences the formation of faith, values, and character formation.

Congregational leaders can get over the imperialism of congregational programs and events as the be-all and end-all of the church.
Leaders must pay attention to their own stories as well as to the Scriptures and the writings of the church over the centuries and millennia.
What really brings the message home is for congregational staff and
boards to tell their own story. They will stop in their tracks in amaze-
ment. They will look at their own list of people and experiences and
say to one another that it is about relationships, it is about family, it is
about daily life experiences (including those in congregations), and it
is about an eclectic array of experiences that simply cannot be limited
to congregational programs and leadership.

The research is there to confirm the importance of the role of personal, trusted relationships in faith formation, especially those relationships experienced in and through one's own home. Recent research
points out that parents are the primary teachers of the faith, but contemporary research tends to get drowned out by institutional assumptions,
experiences, and agenda. Research conducted under the leadership of
Christian Smith at the National Study of Youth and Religion at the
University of North Carolina observes that "parents are normally very
important in shaping the religious and spiritual lives of their teenage
children, even though they may not realize it."[1] The book that discloses
the research goes on to note that "a lot of research in the sociology of
religion suggests that the most important social influence in shaping
young people's religious lives is the religious life modeled and taught
to them by their parents."[2] The book and the research project has been
touted by many in the field of youth ministry and congregational life,
but few pick up on the central theme that parents play a critical role in
the religious and spiritual lives of teens. The external research has not
been enough to grab the attention of leaders in the church, another
example of a church that leads with the Great Omission.

After congregational leaders (leaders can include most every active participant in the ministries of a congregation) have paused and explored their own history of being nurtured in the Christian faith, the next step for them is *not* to throw out the institutional church and its programs and treasured events but to revitalize them. The goal of this book is not to ignore or devalue congregational life but to support it and charge it with the essential additive of personal, trusted relationships. The second book in the Vibrant Faith series, *Vibrant Faith in the Congregation*, will look intently at specific ministries in local congregations and give examples of what those ministries can look like once the church affirms that personal, trusted relationships are rich in divine material for faith formation. With the Vibrant Faith Frame DNA, the possibilities are endless.

> Leaders must pay attention to their own stories as well as to the Scriptures and the writings of the church.

The Other Four Principles

The remaining four principles operate as a consequence of the first principle. The second, "the church is a living partnership between the ministry of the congregation and the ministry of the home," serves as another foundational guide to congregational leadership. *Vibrant Faith in the Congregation* will specify what congregational ministry looks like when the goal is not simply to get people to show up to the congregation but to bring the ministry back to the community and world, often through the lives of people in homes.

The church is a living partnership because of the dynamic relationship between the activities of a congregation and the activities of the homes that are engaged with the congregation. Analogies are most always in danger of breaking down at some point, but a helpful one for the second principle compares the congregation-and-home to grocery store-and-home. The analogy has at least some support from the ancient prayer of the church regarding the holy Scriptures:

Blessed Lord God, you have caused the holy Scriptures to be written for the nourishment of your people. Grant that we may hear them, read, mark, learn and inwardly digest them, that, comforted by your promises, we may embrace and forever hold fast to the hope of eternal life, which you have give us in Jesus Christ, our Savior and Lord. Amen.[3]

The word of God in Scripture is to be digested for the nourishment of the soul, the life of the Christian. In this sense, the congregation and the grocery store both provide important food. The comparison is that the congregation and the grocery store are examples of secondary social systems, meaning that they serve the public by providing resources to be used elsewhere in daily life. The congregation is not an end in itself. It serves a greater good. The same is true of a grocery store. The ultimate goal is not to buy groceries but to eat them. Although it is possible to eat some of the groceries while at the store or to eat at a deli connected with the grocery store, the usual pattern is to buy groceries, take them home, prepare meals, and consume them daily as a source of energy to go about one's daily tasks. It is a dynamic relationship because the two social systems work together. One does not fly down to Central America to buy bananas, then to Iowa or Nebraska to buy corn, then to California to buy grapes, Wisconsin to buy cheese, Washington to buy apples, or Florida to get oranges. They are all made available in the grocery store. The store has become a major provider, a network system of services that get necessary food items and household items into homes. The store is a secondary system that works the commercial network to get provisions accessible to the consumer in the home.

The same is true of a congregation. The congregation offers resources called means of grace, called word and sacrament ministry, and called many other things in different Christian traditions. The goal is not to receive these divine gifts and consume them in the congregation on a Sunday morning before fasting for the week. The intent is to be fed at public worship, public study, public fellowship, and public service and then to take that ministry and those same resources into daily lives to be the church in the world at the office, at school, in the neighborhood, at the scouting event, and in legislative meetings to serve the larger world with the reconciling power of God as ambassadors of God's love in Christ. Unfortunately, for too long the assumption is that Christians are the people who go to worship and to meetings in a Christian building. Christians go to the Christian grocery store (the congregation), eat up, then fast for a few days or weeks and return again to get filled up again.

Pat Keifert has described this in a more detailed way when he identifies four types of congregations. The first is a social or country club, entry by membership only. The second is the gas station and convenience store where people go to get filled up for the moment. The third is the foreign mission congregation where people go to the congregation to worship and to support other people doing ministry on their behalf whether it be across the street or across the globe. Finally, there is the missional congregation that engages those who attend in their own meaningful ministry with others in God's world. The missional congregation is the one that fulfills the biblical mandate to be disciples, not just consumers or promoters. It is the missional congregation that partners the ministry of the congregation with the ministry of the home.[4]

Third Principle

The third principle lives directly out of the second. If the ministry of the home is to be in partnership with the ministry of the congregation, then it must also be true that "where Christ is present in faith, the home is church too." The home, as used here, is more than another location like a congregation's street address; it represents the network of relationships for faith in daily life. The Christian faith is not only nurtured in the home but through the home and back out to the larger world.

As stated above, research over the years has made it quite clear that the home is a critical arena for faith formation. Parents, grandparents, children, siblings, other family, friends, neighbors, and associates have a significant influence in a person's faith, values, character, and lifestyle. It is abundantly evident in the list of influences noted by the staff of the three congregations cataloged above. One sees it in the imitation of a parent by a small child. Words, gestures, and posture are handed down from generation to generation, sometimes with humorous affect, like when a child puts her hands on her hips and then scolds the family pet with a pointed finger. The parent off in the corner wonders, "Do I really look and sound like that?"

Mark DeFries describes the role of the home in *Family Based Youth Ministry*. He was surprised that so many of his youth ministry colleagues quit doing youth ministry, even if they seemed to have very successful youth ministry programs with lots of youth involved (sometimes more than a hundred or two hundred youth). Mark asked his friends why they quit and learned that according to his colleagues, what they were doing was not successful after all. The poster-child youth who came to the youth program off the streets and became the leader of the group would repeatedly disappear once high school was over: end of youth group, end of church experience. It was the youth whose families were also involved in the life of the church who tended to remain in the life of the congregation or some other congregation after high school was over.[5]

Another reason to value the home as church is that forcing people into the congregational church does not work for many people these days. Sometimes the best way to get people into the congregational church is first through the home church. An example of this comes from Richard, who is a pastor on staff in a national church office. He is clearly committed to the life of the public, congregational, and institutional church. For years he has acknowledged that he has been on board "intellectually" with the Vibrant Faith Frame. However, he also now acknowledges that because of a personal friendship and faith quandary, it has moved from intellectual assent to a wholehearted endorsement.

Often pastors become personal priests for family events, much like Father Ralph de Bricassart who served as a kind of family chaplain in *The Thorn Birds*. In Pastor Richard's case, he and his wife have been friends with another couple since the 1970s. At the time, he was a parish pastor, but the friends were not part of any congregation. During those early years of their friendship, the two couples routinely talked about faith, ethics, politics, and parenting. Eventually Richard was asked to baptize their two children, Sarah and Sam. Although this caused some conflict with Richard's commitment to congregational life as foundational, he said yes and baptized the children in the family home. And while the other couple continued to search for the ways to nurture faith in their children, they never fully settled comfortably into a local congregation.

Over the years, Richard continued to wrestle with the question of how to engage his friends most effectively with the Christian life and faith, a faith practice that includes the support of and commitment to an active congregational life. He presided or preached at both of the children's weddings. Then after a few years, he was asked to baptize each of Sarah's two children. Her husband Steve was fully supportive of these two requests.

By the time of the baptism of the second child, Olivia, and with the convictions of the Five Principles, Richard had moved beyond his concerns and perplexity at being a family priest who performs rites to engaging Sarah and Steve with the tools to make the home a place where the church would be alive and well in their lives and their children's lives.

Richard and his wife Naomi met with Sarah and Steve and gave them a FaithChest® (a resource promoted by TYFI that can be a beautiful piece of wooden furniture for the home to fill with faith formation resources) and placed in this box resources to nurture the lives of the children. Richard and Naomi also talked about how Sarah and Steve as Christian parents could participate actively in the life of faith with their baptized children. Sarah has written about this experience in the following way:

> *Olivia's baptism technically happened Saturday June 14, but it started much earlier than that for us, and it lives on day in and day out with the help of our dear friends, the Rev. Richard, who officiated at the ceremony, and his wife Naomi.*

> *Richard and Naomi provided us with a baptism "toolkit" during one of our preparatory meetings. The tool kit was created to help us live the spirit of baptism in our daily lives. The kit contained some bath toys, a children's Bible, a book of*

songs and prayers for our children, and a baptismal manual for Steve and me.

The baptism tool-kit has allowed Steve and me to bring faith and love into the lives of our children in a more purposeful, consistent way. We use the bath toys to talk about the importance of water—and God—in our lives, and we read stories from the children's Bible at bedtime. Mealtime is another opportunity for us to have special conversations about faith, love, and the values that we'd like our children to grow up with. The song and prayer book along with a passed-down family song called, "God's Good Hands," are great conversation starters to help us remember to be thankful for all that we have before us. Each of the items included in the tool-kit have given us simple, meaningful ways to help raise faithful children.

We talked with Richard and Naomi about ways to remind Braden and Olivia (our two children) that they are loved by us and by Jesus as well. One example that stuck out in our minds is to tell them that we love them when we leave their presence for work or an evening. We have done this naturally but now can add, "We love you and Jesus loves you too." Such a simple change in wording but a large change in the amount of love they are reminded they have in their lives.

The baptism itself took place in our backyard and was incredibly special. We used a bowl that had been used in the baptism of Olivia's Grandmother, myself, and her older brother to pour the water on Olivia's head.

It was also quite fitting to hold the ceremony at the place (our home) where all of the education and love we've been talking about above is taking place. We invited our close family and friends who will play leading roles in helping to guide Olivia

(Braden's baptism took place in much the same way) through the ups and downs and challenges she'll face in life.

Richard talked about the importance of making Olivia feel loved despite the messages that our society will send to her over the years. We hope with the community that pledged to help raise her, along with the love, values, and faith that we are now trying to instill upon her every day—she will grow up to be a proud, confident, loving member of society, and we'll always look upon her baptism as one of the cornerstones in seeing that potential become a reality.

Sarah's description of gathering "close family and friends" at Olivia's baptism sounds quite similar to the story of Cornelius, who had "called together his relatives and close friends" (Acts 10:24) to hear the message of Peter. That encounter culminated in the baptisms of Cornelius and the others present. In this case, the gathering began with the teachings of Richard and Naomi and a baptism for Olivia and continues with the language and life of faith for Braden, Olivia, their parents, and the close family and friends.

The Christian message, the presence of Christian disciples, the administration of a sacrament, and the gathering of people for worship and a pledge to live the baptismal life into the future are all signs of the church at work in a home. The hope and expectation is that, just like Cornelius and his family and friends, the family and friends of Olivia will have a lifetime of faith formation in home and congregational contacts. In fact, as Richard has continued his conversations and care for Sarah and her family, he has learned that they are now connecting with a nearby congregation. Sometimes entry and re-entry into a congregation takes a long time. Sometimes the entry begins very explicitly through the home where people like Richard and Naomi walk in with the love of God in Christ for all who dwell there.

The Fourth Principle

The fourth principle, "Faith is caught more than it is taught," can be a real challenge to Christian educators. They sometimes interpret this to mean, "Faith is caught and not taught," but that is not the intent. It is simply that the message taught "comes home," so to speak, through life experiences and the modeling of others. This principle is poignantly portrayed in the Rodney Atkins video *Watchin' You*.[6] For good and ill, Rodney's son sees what his dad does and says and imitates him to an amazing degree. The son is always watching dad and in the process learns more than verbal lessons can ever teach.

> " The Christian faith is not only to be conceived and grasped in the mind; it is to be experienced and lived daily. "

The Fifth Principle

The fifth principle wraps the other principles together with a cross+generational focus: "If we want Christian children and youth, we need Christian adults." The principle operates with a Christian ethic that understands that all Christian adults are Christian parents, thereby making a difference in the lives of children whether or not the adults are the parents of the children. It assumes an ethical approach for Christians: all children are our children. In recent years, it has been suggested that each child should have three to five to seven adults who do not live with that child in the home and yet invest in the child's life in healthy, supportive, and faithful ways. These people include friends of the family, uncles, aunts, coaches, teachers, mentors, and others. Parenting is a community event, not the private activity of a few. Ingvar listed in Congregation C would be one such person.

It is not enough to train children, youth, and young adults in the Christian faith solely through congregational events. The primary caregivers to our children and youth speak volumes about faith and values through their own lives. It is quite true that the reverse is also the case: children and youth impact the faith of the adults around them. But the exception should not be the substitute for the norm. Adults are the adults and, as such, have the role, responsibility, gifts, experience, and wisdom to instruct and guide younger generations in the Christian faith. It is perhaps no more explicitly stated than in Deuteronomy 11:2, "Remember today that it was not your children (who have not known or seen the discipline of the Lord your God), but it is you who must acknowledge his greatness, his mighty hand and his outstretched arm." The text continues with a recitation of the history of the exodus story, the pivotal story of God's redeeming work in the Old Testament. That experience and that story serve as the heart of the message to be conveyed in word and deed to the next generations. Similarly, the life experiences and stories of adults in the church serve as the heart of the message to be conveyed in word and deed to the next generations of Christians.

The Four Keys

The Christian faith is not only to be conceived and grasped in the mind; it is to be experienced and lived daily. In *Growing Up Religious,* Robert Wuthnow observes,

> Effective religious socialization comes about through embedded practices; that is, through specific, deliberate religious activities that are firmly intertwined with the daily habits of family routines, of eating and sleeping, of having conversations, of adorning the spaces in which people live, of celebrating the holidays, and of being part of a community.[7]

According to Wuthnow, people are brought into the Christian life and faith through activities that are woven into the flow of daily life. He calls such activities "embedded practices." He goes on to point out, "Compared with these practices, the formal teachings of religious leaders often pale in significance. Yet, when such practices are present, formal teachings also become more important."[8] What Wuthnow asserted in 1999, the Search Institute had also studied and published in 1990 when their research concluded, "Of the two strongest connections to faith maturity, family religiousness is slightly more important than lifetime exposure to Christian education."[9] The more succinct list of faith practices noted by that study included "the frequency with which an adolescent talked with mother and father about faith, the frequency of family devotions, and the frequency with which parents and children together were involved in efforts, formal or informal, to help other people."[10] At the heart of effective Christian education, effective Christian faith formation, and effective "religious socialization" is not the classroom but a lifestyle that includes specific faith practices, especially those in the home.

These research studies and that of others led to the identification of four foundational or "embedded" practices called the Four Keys: caring conversations, devotions, service, and rituals and traditions. Those foundational activities in daily life present, teach, reinforce, and stabilize the Christian life in certain faith, values, assumptions, and lifestyle. The Four Keys represent the irreducible practices out of which more complex faith-forming and faith-grounded activities occur.

The Four Keys include the practices in which all individuals and homes engage. They are not necessarily Christian practices (for example, Wuthnow's work studies Christian and Jewish life). What makes them Christian is that they are lived and experienced "in Christ." Conversations take place in a variety of settings and fit a variety of interpersonal occasions. The devotional life represents most anything that expresses what individuals and households believe in, or put another way, how the family practices the sense of the divine in their lives, even if the divine is equated with money, prestige, security, or a more traditional religious orientation. This takes place in formal settings like a table grace at mealtime or nighttime prayer as children are put to bed. It can also occur in more informal settings like watching a sunrise or sunset and marveling at God's creative beauty.

Women can practice a devotional life at a baby shower when they want to offer something spiritual and give the mother-to-be words of wisdom, inspiration, humor, and hope. The devotional component of one recent baby shower included a gift of a votive candle given to each participant with the commitment of all those attending the baby shower to light the candle and say a prayer or offer thoughts when the woman goes to the hospital to deliver the baby. Again, this devotional practice need not be Christian. What makes it a Christian practice is the prayers offered as part of the Christian faith and the candles lit in remembrance of the light of Christ.

Service, one of the Four Keys and an essential component of a community's survival is expressed in Wuthnow's list in the language of "being part of a community." Much of his list also fits the category of rituals and traditions, those things that families do routinely or that groups of people do to adorn "the space in which people live" or to celebrate holidays and other occasions.

The Four Keys offer the distinct, inseparable, and irreducible practices of survival and meaning in which humans must engage. These four practices become arranged in a rich variety of ways to develop more elaborate, historic Christian practices like Christian hospitality, stewardship of the earth, evangelism, worship, hospice care, and much more. The Four Keys are invaluable because the other more numerous and elaborate Christian practices cannot be used very effectively to offer leadership for a congregation or a home. Members of the home or congregational church cannot recall an entire list of twelve or twenty Christian practices to order one's daily life and community life. The Four Keys are simply four practices that can be remembered, and they can guide and shape the church in the home and the church in the congregation.

The Four Keys also benefit from the fact that they are not the language or experience of a particular denomination or socio-economic group. They describe what is common to all. As one black, Pentecostal, inner-city leader stated, "These are the kinds of things we do to survive as a church and community." An Episcopal priest observed that the Four Keys are another way of talking about the Benedictine spirituality used by the Episcopal church, practices that focus on obedience, stability, and conversion of life. The Four Keys have proven themselves to be doable, replicable, teachable, and translatable so that individuals, households, congregations, and larger church bodies can guide their ministries on the basis of these essential and distinct yet inseparable Christian actions.

The language of the Four Keys may be contemporary, but the practices have a long history. They are evident in the historic language of the church. One of the Prayers of the Day for Ash Wednesday reads, "Merciful God, accompany our journey through these forty days. Renew us by our baptism to provide for those who are poor, to pray for those in need, and to fast from self-indulgence, that we may find our treasures in the life of your Son, Jesus Christ, our Savior and Lord . . ."[11] Prayerfully seeking the treasured life in Christ describes the devotional life. Caring for the poor and others in need gives a good example of service. Avoiding greed is reflected in the Christian ritual and tradition of fasting. All of this is expressed in language of a prayer that itself gives words and ideas to be communicated with others, a script for caring conversations. The clarity is simple. The execution, of course, is not. Between those two sentences resides the life of a Christian.

AAA Christian Disciples

Christian discipleship is the divine work that moves in and through the Five Principles of a vibrant faith and the Four Key faith practices. That discipleship is described in the language of AAA: authentic, available, and affirming.

An authentic Christian is real—not perfect but honest, not deceitful but candid, not hidden and always a sinner while redeemed as a saint. The authentic Christian is most of all free to serve, free to believe and trust God, free to live, free to love, and free to fail at it all. The authentic Christian lives with grace and mercy and peace that passes all human understanding, and, therefore, is available to and affirming of others.

The Apostle Peter embodies the authentic life of the Christian. Peter said he would never turn away from his Lord, but he did. Three times he denied Jesus at the time one would have hoped Peter would have been most present, courageous, and the ideal follower. Instead, he was just a real flesh-and-blood follower. The authentic Christian disappoints oneself and others too. The authentic Christian stands not by human strength. In the midst of human frailty, including doubt and despair, the authentic Christian lives by the power of grace and mercy.

An available disciple is one who seeks to be present and aware of the needs of others and creation. An available disciple does not pray to escape the world but to be more fully invested in God's world (see the

Six Locations of Ministry). Prayer and action make a disciple available to be a tool of God's work and will for the world, a true servant, even a slave of God. Jesus describes the available disciple as one who feeds the hungry, gives a cup of water to the thirsty, welcomes the stranger, clothes the naked, visits the sick and imprisoned (see Matthew 25:31-40).

An affirming Christian does not profess "I'm okay, you're okay." Rather, in the midst of sin, death, and evil, the affirming Christian believes that God's word gets the last word, and it is a word of hope; it relies on God's undeserved kindness; it envisions the promise of a new heaven and a new earth. Affirming Christians know how to say, "Thank you," "I'm sorry," "I forgive you," and "Let me help." It's the voice and pen of Paul who stated, "I thank my God every time I remember you, constantly praying with joy in every one of my prayers for all of you, because of your sharing in the gospel from the first day until now. I am confident of this, that the one who began a good work among you will bring it to completion by the day of Jesus Christ" (Philippians 1:3-6).

These three characteristics summarize the intent of the work of the church: Christian discipleship. Every congregational committee and board, every Christian mentor, elder, or parent would do well to remember that what God calls us to be are faithful followers of Jesus, people who are AAA Christian disciples.

The Need to Repent of the Great Omission

The Broader Quandary

The Great Omission of the church is the loss of what "family" or "home" life offers in the shaping of the Christian faith, both in terms of beliefs and as a way of life. This has occurred within the larger culture, where the role of the home has been compromised. Therefore, this view has become so pervasive within society that church leaders are not always aware of the bias. Many church leaders are not aware of a problem with ignoring the role of the home in nurturing the Christian faith. They may not be mindful, for example, of the fact that resources like Luther's Small Catechism, written for the home, for the head of the household, were never meant simply as a piece of curriculum for a classroom. They were designed for family use at the dinner table, at the bedside, and all of the other places where faith is shaped in the home.

Family life has at times been reduced to the role of shelter, providing physical nourishment and emotional support. The assumption is that everything else that an individual needs for a meaningful life can be provided by a more public and institutional setting: education through school systems, health care through clinics and hospitals, a sense of value through employment and a paycheck from the workplace, entertainment through TicketMaster and downloads, and of course, faith from congregation, mosque, synagogue, or temple.

Twentieth-century America replaced an inherent value of family life with the value of institutional life. It has been said that twentieth-century America became an "expert- ridden system."[1] These experts reside in publicly acknowledged institutions: doctors and nurses in hospital and clinics; judges, lawyers, and police officers in the judicial system; professors and teachers in colleges, universities, and schools; pastors and elders in congregations; and other experts in service organizations, foundations, and think tanks.

In an expert-ridden system, one has little to say unless that person is the expert. Since parents are not seen as experts, they might think that they have little to say, even about their own children. When my wife Gloria was one, her mother noticed her sitting in the high chair and swinging only one leg. Her mother determined she also had a fever. She rushed to the phone and called the family doctor believing that Gloria had polio. Without much other information, the doctor was able to respond on the phone, "Mrs. Fry, you are an overanxious mother. Gloria most likely has a cold. Give her aspirin and send her to bed." In 1954, doctors were the kinds of experts who could pontificate where parents could not. Gloria, it was discovered later, had polio. To the doctor's credit, he was later known to show up at the Fry home unannounced to check in on and care for Gloria. Even in "expert-ridden" eras, compassion and sensibility can find a way.

Harper Lee's *To Kill a Mockingbird* portrays life in the Deep South in the 1930s, but in some ways the book reflects the larger culture and a longer history as well. When Scout Finch begins her first day of school, the teacher, Miss Caroline, discovers that Scout, a precocious little girl in many respects, already knows how to read. Miss Caroline assumes that Scout's father, Atticus Finch, taught Scout to read at home. She says to Scout,

"Now you tell your father not to teach you anymore. It's best to begin reading with a fresh mind. You tell him I'll take over from here and try to undo the damage—'"
"Ma'am?"
'Your father does not know how to teach. You can have a seat now."[2]

That is how it was in much of twentieth-century America generally. Parents were not valued. Parents were not the experts. Parents were to let others raise their children. Miss Caroline simply expressed the assumptions of the day. She was the teacher and Scout's father was not.

A more recent example of institutions replacing families comes from an observation from a national church staff member. The individual could not support the work of The Youth & Family Institute because its mission was misguided. That person said that the church could not focus attention on families because they are so dysfunctional. Clearly that has been the attitude of more than one church leader. As we see later in the chapter, it represents a sentiment that allows an otherwise wise and faithful church leader to observe that Jesus didn't have the least interest in the family.

Dysfunction is a rather difficult charge to address, because we all have it. It is called sin, brokenness, imperfection, and so on. Dysfunction is a psychological (expert) term for what we can biblically and theologically refer to as sin. What human community is not beset by sin or dysfunction? What about the dysfunction of congregations? We know there are dysfunctional congregations all around us, but our church leaders and many others refuse to give up on them. Just as there are a number of congregations doing wonderful ministry (with an array of dysfunction in their midst), so too many families are caring for children, the elderly, neighbors, and strangers in the midst of the dysfunctions of everyday relationships.

The Great Omission is discerned no more clearly than in a recent comment made by a nationally known theologian and church leader who stated at a clergy conference with over two thousand present, "I don't think Jesus gave a rip about the family." That comment represents a bias that has shaped congregational leadership in many church circles in recent decades. It is defended by the same two or three misunderstood quotes from Jesus in the New Testament. This constant referral to the same two or three Bible passages ought to cause some concern and question. The interpretations of these biblical passages are corroborated by the intellectual and social bias inherited from much of twentieth-century American culture.

The statement "I don't think Jesus gave a rip about the family" articulates a bias that most people do not even recognize as a bias. The audience laughed aloud at the pontification, joining the speaker in deriding any other notion. But this preconceived notion goes largely unchallenged by a large segment of the church.

> We were the first genera-
> tion to understand personal
> development in civilization
> without the family as a basic
> building block.

Home Life in the Twentieth Century

The twentieth century experienced a number of movements and social realities that challenged the role of parents and the value of family life. It began with the hopes and expectations that the social and natural sciences were now advanced enough to end diseases, poverty, and war. In such an optimistic climate, the efforts of public, institutional life like public education and public health services were emerging as the better provider than the home for the needs of children in a modern world. When that dream was compromised[3] by the realities of an early twentieth-century recession and then the Great Depression, by the crime and decay of the Roaring Twenties with its gangsters and speakeasies, and by World War I and continued international tensions thereafter, the self-realization movement emerged. It articulated a social and psychological creed that decried any outside voice of authority, including the voice of government, church, and parents over the independent voice of the self. The predominance of each individual was not answerable to social standards, whatever they may be. The self was to be spontaneous, free to live and to love by one's own standards. It was a movement that was at times uncritically and unwittingly endorsed by the church. Its language and assumptions about what it is to be an individual self even crept into seminary education through the field of pastoral theology. In such a setting, parents with children in the home lost social capital and sense of importance.

Other historical events contributed to the devaluation of family life. World War II and the economic boom that followed fostered a mobility that sent even more people away from family farms and into factories and cities, separating parents and children from grandparents and other family members (often the unofficial "parent educators" of the day). The social and geographic mobility, televisions in the homes (the advertising arm of consumerism), increased materialism, increased housing costs, increasing divorce rates, the Vietnam War, the prevalence of drugs, the sexual revolution, children and families living in poverty or without affordable health care, and latchkey and daycare children all took their toll on family life. As a consequence of these factors and others, by the 1980s America was said to have "virulent anti-family sentiments."[4] The assumption was that family life was falling apart. In endorsing Dolores Curran's 1984 book Traits of a Healthy Family, a Christian writer states, "Few of us need more critiques of what is wrong with families."[5] Even when a book like Curran's became available to buttress the family, it could be framed with a negative spin on the family.

By the 1980s it was observed that, at the time, we were the first generation to understand personal development in civilization without the family as a basic building block.[6] Development jumped from the contributions of each individual to the social matrix of public life. The devaluation of family in the twentieth century was paralleled by the ascendancy of public institutions. One has trouble being an expert or having an expert opinion or being an expert witness without a recognized institution to certify one's expertness.

As a result, in the twentieth-century church, the life of the home and the larger realm of personal, trusted relationships took a back seat to the life of the public, organized church in the congregation. This is best illustrated in the book *God Is in the Small Stuff.* The book, published in 1998, offers the vantage point of an end-of-the-century perspective. In the chapter describing the church, the authors note, "When the apostle Paul wrote about the church, he wasn't talking about a building, an activity, or an institution. For Paul, the expression of *church* meant a personal relationship among Christians."[7] The authors seem to get the emphasis presented here. But at the end of their chapter, the two authors offer suggestions on how to be involved in the life of the church, and every example (eleven in all) are about the public, congregational expression of the church. They suggest, "Get involved at church," although earlier they state that "church" is not primarily a place. They go on to encourage people to participate actively in Sunday worship, tolerate church leaders, give money, teach Sunday school, and on and on. None of the suggestions in and of themselves is objectionable. It is simply uncanny how predictable the cultural DNA is on institutional life. Even when authors think they are critical of the language of institution, they bend over backward to support only the institutional dimension of church. The predominance of the concept of church as an organization one supports is so insidious, so pervasive, that those who challenge the concept fall prey to it anyway.

Jesus as a Family-Friendly Guy

It is important to pause here to explore how the church could imagine such a limited mission for the home. The formula for this perspective involves the cultural bias against the family described above as an interpretive lens for a few New Testament passages.

It is interesting that those who besmirch the role of the home do so on the basis of the same two or three Bible passages. The primary passages are Mark 3:33-35 (see also Matthew 12:48-50 and Luke 8:21) and Matthew 10:34-39 (see also Luke 12:51-53; 14:26). Sometimes a third passage is included to verify Jesus' opposition to family: Luke 9:59-62.

And he [Jesus] replied, "Who are my mother and my brothers?" And looking at those who sat around him, he said, "Here are my mother and my brothers! Whoever does the will of God is my brother and sister and mother. (Mark 3:33-35)

"Do not think that I [Jesus] have come to bring peace to the earth; I have not come to bring peace, but a sword. For I have come to set a man against his father, and a daughter against her mother and a daughter-in-law against her mother-in-law; and one's foes will be members of one's own household. Whoever loves father or mother more than me is not worthy of me; and whoever loves son or daughter more than me is not worthy of me; and whoever does not take up the cross and follow me is not worthy of me. Those who find their life will lose it, and those who lose their life for my sake will find it." (Matthew 10:34-39)

To another he [Jesus] said, "Follow me." But he said, "Lord, first let me go and bury my father." But Jesus said to him, "Let the dead bury their own dead; but as for you, go and proclaim the kingdom of God." Another said, "I will follow you, Lord; but let me first say farewell to those at my home." Jesus said to him, "No one who puts a hand to the plow and looks back is fit for the kingdom of God." (Luke 9:59-62)

First of all, before looking at Jesus' views of family, we must note that comparing Jesus' words with the contemporary "family" is something of a misnomer. In the Hebrew and Greek languages of the Old and New Testament, there is no word for "family" as we use it today. From the biblical perspective the word "household" might better describe a variety of intimate communities of care, support, and training that nurture people's lives within the local culture. For example, one biblical scholar has identified forty different types of such families or households.[8] The focus is really about the trusted relationships we rely on over time that give us identity, purpose, meaning, and a sense of personal and social wellbeing. In these various communities of care, support, and guidance, children and adults navigate the larger world around them. These family groupings transmit—pass along—language, values, commitments, religious convictions and practices, and skills to survive in the larger social system economically, politically, and religiously.

Yes, there are passages in the Gospels that can be interpreted to imply that Jesus is against the family, especially with today's cultural bias toward the family. But no, that is not Jesus' point in these passages. In Matthew 10:34-39, it is not that Jesus is against the family; he simply makes it clear that family life is such a faith-forming community that to follow him would mean a serious rift with other family members who remained faithful to another religious identity, in this case the Jewish faith. Jesus describes the result of following him. It will divide faith-forming communities called "families" or "households." The result means that Jesus' presence and work on behalf of the reign of God brings a dividing sword, not peace: "For I have come to set a man against his father, and a daughter against her mother, and a daughter-in-law against her mother-in-law; and one's foes will be members of one's own household" (Matthew 10:35-36).

It is true. Faith is such a core piece to family life, the life of a household, that to take a different religious stance, to take a different faith, will divide homes. We see this in John 9. The man born blind is alienated from his parents. They are unwilling to come to his aid when the Pharisees come to them to learn if, indeed, their son was born blind, an important issue against the miraculous deed of Jesus giving him sight. The parents refuse to come to the aid of their son because they fear they "would be put out of the synagogue" (John 9:22), a technical term like being excommunicated. They would be without their religious moorings, so they sacrificed their son. It became a divided family.

Jesus' point is that even when the breach in family life occurs, one cannot let the highly valued life of the household undermine one's life in Christ: "Whoever loves father or mother more than me is not worthy of me" (Matthew 10:37a). Luke makes the intended point abundantly clear, especially clear for twentieth- and twenty-first-century

American eyes and ears: "'Whoever comes to me and does not hate father and mother, wife and children, brothers and sisters, yes, and even life itself, cannot be my disciple" (Luke 14:26).

It is interesting that those who say Jesus is against the family do not go on to say that Jesus is against us, against our own lives. Of course Jesus is not against us, nor is he against the family. To follow Jesus is an ultimate commitment exceeding even our commitment to our own survival and way of life independent from Jesus. These texts use the wisdom rhetoric of hyperbole. Jesus speaks as a sage, even as the wisdom of God. Jesus makes a dramatic statement to make an even more dramatic point: life lived in faith in Jesus is not about an ultimate loyalty to Jesus and our family, or Jesus and our personal wellbeing, or Jesus and our national loyalty, or Jesus and our loyalty to our congregation or denomination, or Jesus and our love for our favorite sports team, or Jesus and our commitment to our financial success, or Jesus and our commitment to anything. Jesus alone is Savior and Lord. He does not need help from any other form of meaning and value for our lives to be meaningful and valuable. Through—not alongside—Jesus all else gains its importance and role in our lives.

Again, when Jesus says, "'Here are my mother and my brothers! Whoever does the will of God is my brother and sister and mother," (Mark 3:34b-35) he is not denying the role of family, he is expanding it. In fact, Jesus here articulates a larger, less exclusive and isolated sense of family than contemporary church and culture assume. It has been said that blood is thicker than water, but Jesus here is insinuating (Christian baptism in the church is not yet happening) that water (baptismal water) is thicker than blood. This is not a bad thing, and it is certainly not against the family. However, with an anti-family bias, it becomes such an easy text to use.

A recent biographical example may help here. On June 13, 2008, newsman and public icon Tim Russert died suddenly at age fifty-eight. As political analyst and the voice and face for years for Meet the Press, he was beloved and admired by a wide swath of celebrities, politicians, and the larger masses of America. In a tribute to his life, Jim Wallis, Editor-in-Chief and CEO of Sojourners, writes the following:

> Tim Russert was not only the premier political journalist in America, as everyone agreed but was also a real "father figure" to many people, from the whole family at NBC News to the extended community of journalists in this city—even to many of his rivals. And so many of Russert's colleagues and friends spoke of his interest in their children and how much he meant in the lives of their own families.... Tim Russert is a role model for every dad and mom; every uncle, aunt, godparent, teacher, and coach; and every adult who realizes how much kids need people to love and teach them the important things of life."[9]

Here we have a biographical description that lifts up the larger sense of family referenced in Mark 3. The tribute also identifies a dedication to committed relationships that nurture the lives of others, especially children and youth. This represents part of the rich soil the church needs to be the witness of God's presence and love in and for the world through Christ Jesus.

The same news article described Russert as a man for whom faith and family loomed large in his life. This is also consistent with a man who wrote a best-selling book on his father.[10] According to Jim Wallis's accolades quoted above, Tim Russert got what Jesus and the historic church know: you don't have to be family by marriage, birth, or adoption to be family to others. It is a treasured discovery.

Two other observations about the accolades laid upon Tim Russert are worth noting. First, there are a lot of Tim Russerts in the world; they are just not nationally known names. Like Tim's story, sometimes the stories of individuals who care for others are not told publicly until they die. What follows is the story told by a Christian education director about a couple in a congregation she once served:

> *I never had the opportunity to meet him, but I know that he cared about kids and that he was serious about passing on his faith. I was told that each Sunday, he attended the 11:00 a.m. worship service with a pocket or two full of "dum-dum" lollipops. Every child, most teenagers, a host of college students, and even a few adults found him before or after worship each*

week to get their candy treat, "check-in" with him, and share their life stories. Although he had never been taught the Five Principles of what it means to be the church or the Four Keys for nurturing faith, he shared his faith through trusted personal relationships in the congregation where he worshipped.

By the time I was called to serve that congregation, he had already joined the host of saints in the church triumphant and his wife had taken over the lollipop ministry. Each week I witnessed the children of God, of all ages and life stages, seek her out to get a lollipop, say hello, and share their stories with her. I heard preschoolers share the news of a new puppy with her or give her a picture they had colored. I watched families with elementary aged children take her to lunch. The youth and their parents raked her leaves every fall; the college students sang Christmas carols each December. And as she aged, various adults and families brought her to worship or other events hosted by the congregation. When she passed away and we were making plans for the funeral service, the senior pastor asked me to go to the store and buy the biggest bag of "dum-dums" I could find and put it in the pulpit. At the end of his sermon, he asked the congregation who was going to take over this very important ministry task, and we had lots of volunteers. Everybody was willing to volunteer for this seemingly simple, but very important job![11]

This beloved couple also knew what it meant to see others as family and to be an adult who cared for children of all ages. It expressed a sense of family that many others wanted to emulate.

A second point is that there are many who could, with a little bit of encouragement, experience, and modeling, be the kind of "family" mentors mentioned above. What follows is the account given by a man who attended one of Vibrant Faith Ministries congregational trainings called Hand in Hand. Part of the weekend experience is a cross+generational activity that allows children, youth, and adults of various ages to be together and support one another with personal stories that often become faith stories. At the end of the weekend event, he wrote an unsolicited email to TYFI regarding his reaction to the Hand in Hand and in particular the cross+generational activity. He started by explaining briefly his life in and out of the church. He returned to the church eight or nine years ago because of the efforts of his daughter (an example of the power of family living a vibrant faith). After mentioning his daughter's influence and his participation on church council, he continued,

> *Unfortunately, or more likely fortunately, God sent yet another messenger to further define my mission. Enter [the TYFI staff member]. In the short time you spent with us this weekend, my commitment and passion has been further defined. Trust me when I tell you that after twenty-eight years as a police officer, cynicism becomes an integral part of one's being. The last thing that I wanted to do was deal with kids. I raised two of my own, a son and a daughter. [My wife] serves as a confirmation guide, and I have been asked several times to do the same. Needless to say, I have not answered the call, thinking that I have nothing to contribute, nor would I have anything meaningful to say to someone of that age.*

> *This morning, I found that as usual, I was wrong. The time spent with our youth this morning was an epiphany. Not only did I see them reach out in our game, but in the small group discussions, I found that I actually did have something to contribute, and they in fact wanted to hear what I had to say.*

> *I'm looking forward to becoming more involved with these wonderful young people and plan on at least volunteering for the mentor program, if not jumping in with both feet as a confirmation guide.*

> *My wife and I have also engaged in meaningful conversation since yesterday on levels that we've not approached before.*

It's difficult to explain, but I feel a difference in our relationship that was not present three days ago as we have discussed our walk with Christ on a deeper level than we previously have.

I have already thanked God for sending you to us. I would again like to thank you for being here and sharing your time and talents with us. I'm convinced that our paths did not cross by coincidence. God put you into my life to further strengthen my walk in faith, and further direct his plans for me.

Thank you so very much, and add me to the list of people whose lives you have profoundly touched. I'm sure the list is long. May God bless you and your continuing work.[12]

This man gives testimony to the power of experience and the power of preconceived ideas about his gifts and abilities and about the interests of another generation. He also indicates that the weekend experience resulted in more than a new interest in youth. It resulted in a renewed and deepened faith life for him and his wife. His understanding of the family of God widened and his appreciation of his own marriage deepened.

In addition to the two Bible passages referenced above, a third biblical reference is sometimes used as evidence for Jesus' opposition to family. It describes the challenge to would-be disciples. A man says he will follow Jesus but first needs to bury his father. Another simply wants to say good-bye to those at his home. Jesus responds, "Let the dead bury their own dead," and "No one who puts a hand to the plow and looks back is fit for the kingdom of God" (Luke 9:60, 62). Again, Jesus' words can be seen as devaluing the family, or it can be understood as a wise sage using hyperbole to make the point that those loyalties and events that seem so important pale by comparison to following Jesus. Jesus stands alone as the source of meaning and conduct in life.

The idea that Jesus is against the family also stands in opposition to Jesus' own life and other testimony from the biblical church. Jesus valued his own family life so much that from the cross he made sure his own mother would be taken care of after his death (see John

19:26-27). The New Testament church did not understand Jesus' words as being indifferent to or opposed to family life. Not to take care of the needs of individual family members is to deny "the faith and is worse than an unbeliever" (1 Timothy 5:8). Colossians 3:12-17 offers a beautiful description of the baptismal life (baptism was referenced in Colossians 2:12 and in the baptismal imagery of "clothe yourselves" in 3:12). The very next passage does not continue by describing this baptismal journey in the public experience of church but in the domestic life of faith in the home (3:18-25), the family life of antiquity that included husbands and wives, parents and children, and masters and slaves. These biblical references are left out, of course, when one argues that Jesus is against or doesn't give a rip about home and family.

This devaluing of the role of the home seems at times to be in the water we drink and the air we breathe. It makes it so easy to disengage from the role of the home as an arena in which to live a vibrant faith that expresses the abundant life in Christ. It makes it so easy to distance the ministry of the church from engaging with the roles of children, siblings, parents, grandparents, neighbors, friends, and even the stranger we meet. That cultural water and air we take in compromises the life and work of the church.

" This is an exciting time to be part of the church. "

More than the Institutional Church

Let's be very clear here: this critique is not against the institutional church. The critique offered here is that it is so very difficult for us to see more than the institutional side of church life. This book is about that "more." In fact, this book is in support of the health of the institutional church, its leadership, and its programs by noting that we dare not put all our eggs in the institutional church basket. It is not fair to congregational leaders. It is not fair to our evaluations of the programs. God also works outside the "God-box" institution to nurture a vibrant faith in the lives of individuals, households, and larger communities. If we fail to recognize God's work of creating faith in all areas of life, then we end up asking too much of pastors, Christian educators, other congregational leaders, and the programs they support. One must wonder how much more could be done if we did a more thorough job of partnering the ministry of the congregation with the ministry of the home.

We have a ways to go to recapture the trust, confidence, and willingness of parents (and grandparents, godparents, and other caregivers) to own their God-given role as faith mentors in their own homes. In subtle but significant ways we have told parents for decades that they do not have a lot to offer (except maybe as a taxi driver or chaperone). We as the identified church leadership need to be willing to say, when appropriate, "The sin is ours for neglecting and undermining your role as spiritual leaders in your own homes. We will need to go slowly and with care to change that history. What we do know is that you, the parents, are by far more influential than pastors, Sunday school teachers, and catechists to pass on the Christian faith to your children. If together we want to establish a meaningful ministry in this place, then your participation is essential. Let's find ways for you to gain courage, strategies, and resources that will help you as parents reclaim your rightful place as 'apostles, bishops, and priests'[13] in your own homes."

The Pivotal Role of the Great Omission in Church Renewal

Many congregational leaders are seeking a faithful and biblical renewal of the church. It is now time for these same leaders and congregations to look closely at the church's Great Omission and the recovery of the role of the home. These are the leaders and congregations that will reach out to children and youth because they are God's too and because these people keep the church honest and open to the real questions of real lives. These leaders and congregations will reach out to family life in ways that help people daily address issues of life and faith in homes, at the office, or in the fields. These leaders and congregations will draw the old and the young together to learn and grow together. They will draw new saints and seasoned saints together to live and to be energized together by a world that needs the message of grace, mercy, and peace to all of the world's experiences and for all of our days. These leaders and congregations will be increasingly open to homes and families of different shapes and sizes to welcome in the reign of God together.

This is an exciting time to be part of the church. To the credit of church leaders across the country and in various church bodies, a passionate concern for renewal has reemerged. Discipleship is gaining momentum over membership. Meaningful ministry is taking precedence over attendance numbers. Clearly, the church needs to hear the words of Jesus in the Great Commission of Matthew 28:16-20. At the same time the church needs to address the Great Omission in the church in recent decades. Addressing the one will help in hearing the other.

4

UNDERSTANDING AND MERCY FOR PARENTS AND CAREGIVERS

An Active Role in the Lives of Our Children

In the 1960s a study of fifty active United Presbyterian families in Denver discovered that the parents were reluctant to assert their parental influence fearing alienation through their misuse of power. The research identified a widespread insecurity and role confusion on the part of parents that has emerged in the United States in the last half of the twentieth century. Parents have avoided imposing on their children a disciplinary or teaching position, even in the areas of Christian faith and values. It is not uncommon to hear parents say about their child's faith life, "I will let my child decide for herself."

Reflecting on this research as well as other data collected at that time, one author in the field of Christian parenting concluded, "The modern Protestant parent is not comfortable in the position of authority and the arbiter of discipline in the family."[1] That was more than four decades ago, and not much has changed. Although there are some encouraging signs on the horizon, by and large parents still feel anxious about what role of authority they play in their children' lives. They remain uncertain about what they can say and what they can model for their young.

It may be this very lack of clarity for the authoritative (not authoritarian) role of parents in the lives of their own children that encourages some parents to chauffeur their children around to every coach, instructor, guide, director, and guru that they can find. The ridiculously busy lives of many children and youth before and after school and during the summers may reflect the fear of parents that they have little substance to offer their own kids. These parents travel the world around them to give their kids what many assume they cannot give themselves: life-giving skills, insights, values, and faith. The contemporary model of surrogate parenting (through coaches, other children, and youth leaders) and overscheduled children may be further evidence of a culture that has devalued the role of parents for decades and even generations.

Interestingly, back in Denver in 2008 and during an open discussion with participants near the end of a conference led by TYFI, one mother concluded, "I may not know everything, but I do know enough to say something." The crowd cheered. She summarized so well the sentiments of many other parents (and grandparents, godparents, and other caregivers to children and youth) present in the room. She was referring to her newly found confidence to speak and live her faith in her own home and with her own children. Prior to what she learned at the conference, she had surmised that she had very little, if anything, to say to her children about the Christian faith. All she knew was that she didn't know much. The contents of that conference— reflecting a confession of the church's Great Omission and what to do about it—gave her awareness, insight, and strategies to apply to the faith life of her own home the same kinds of awareness, insight, and strategies that congregations can offer parents every week.

This new-found confidence and courage to be an engaged parent in one's own home is nothing new. In the 1960s, Vatican II reaffirmed that the home was the "domestic church." For those who are the theological beneficiaries of the Reformation, it represents a rediscovery of what the Protestant church has known for centuries. Martin Luther honored mothers and fathers in 1522 as "apostles, bishops, and priests to their children, for it is they who make them acquainted with the gospel. In short, there is no greater or nobler authority on earth than that of parents over their children, for this authority is both spiritual and temporal."[2] Here the Reformer does not chide parents (he can do that too) but elevates them with the status of great honor. He had a clear understanding of the value—the God-given value (not consumer value based on niche marketing of what kids want parents to buy them)—of parents in the lives of children and in the life of church and society. Luther wrote in the preface to a volume of his home postils (sermons for the home), "These sermons were preached by me at certain times in my dwelling, in the presence of my household, that I, as the head of the family, might do my duty toward them, by instructing them how to lead a Christian life."[3] Luther did not preach and teach to his children and others who lived in or visited his home because he was a pastor, professor, or doctor of theology. He did so because he was a parent. This biographical affirmation of the role of the home is in no small part why Luther wrote the Small Catechism, for the instruction of the Christian faith in the home. Luther understood the critical role and authority of parents—of both mothers and fathers—as apostles, bishops, and priests in the lives of their children and in the life of the church.

Luther's Small Catechism was written for the home, but in congregations that use the Small Catechism today (most Lutheran congregations, some Evangelical Free and Covenant congregations, and others who have a heritage that connects them to the Reformation theology of Martin Luther), one would think that Luther wrote the Catechism as a parish curriculum, a primary tool to harass teenagers in a classroom. A recent book on the role of the church as an evangelizing community states, "Resources like the Small Catechism were to be put into the hands of every Christian to prepare them for a life of faith and witness in the world."[4] This statement misses the role of parents and the home environment as major contributors to Christian instruction and evangelism. The perspective of that contemporary book on evangelism routinely moves from a focus on individuals to congregations, jumping right over the role of the home as a basic building block of faith, values, and character formation.

Many congregations today that study and promote Luther's teachings do not associate his writings with the importance of the home. No wonder parents feel so hesitant to take an active role in the faith life of their own children. The church for years has implied by its rhetoric that parents do not have such a role.[5] At the same time, I have worked with numerous congregations whose staff and other leaders routinely express frustrations with parents for "not doing their job" in the faith nurturing of their own children. Parents find themselves in a double bind. On the one hand, little preaching and teaching we hear truly esteems the home and communicates deep respect and awe for the role of parents in the faith life of children. On the other hand, parents are judged for not doing enough, which often translates into not getting their kids to congregational programs (preferably, on time). In the midst of this church culture of the Great Omission, how can leaders turn around and accuse parents of not doing their job? Is it not time for the repentance of the church regarding its neglect of parents and other primary caregivers of children and youth?

This sensitivity toward and support of parents is also important to those who are reading this book, many of whom are likely parents themselves. Parents reading this book are either consciously or subconsciously aware—probably painfully so—of what in most instances has not happened in their own homes. It makes little difference if the reader is pastor, other staff member, elder, council president, or committee chair. The level of engagement with the Christian faith in the home has little to do with one's role in congregational leadership and much more to do with the kind of modeling and encouragement they have received from valued mentors in their own lives.

> " Luther's Small Catechism was written for the home. "

The Good News about Parents

The important observation for all of us in the church is that, given encouragement, training, and resources, parents can and do rise to the occasion, like that mother at the conference in Denver. In fact, many have been waiting (whether they knew it or not) for help to come. Kristen A. G. Venne did her doctoral research on the Vibrant Faith Frame (primarily the Five Principles, Four Keys, and Milestones Ministry, a cross+generational faith formation program that utilizes the Five Principles and Four Keys) and conducted the research in three congregations that had been working closely with TYFI. Each congregation was at a different stage of development with the work of the Institute. Venne interviewed staff and adult members from each of the three congregations. In one focus group interview, a mother offered the following assessment:

> My husband and I are in a unique situation that we've raised almost two different families because we have a blended family. And we can see clearly the difference between our two older children and our two younger children. . . . [W]hen we were raising the older children, the church didn't equip us with any tools. We were kind of winging it on our own; we were trying our best but we weren't taught the kinds of things we are being taught now. You know those Four Keys, caring conversation, ritual and traditions; we had some of those things because we both grew up Lutheran, in traditional Lutheran homes, so we had a little bit of those tools, but nothing like we have now. And we can really see now the difference in curiosity, and the questions they ask, in the openness that they have.[6]

Venne's study records how parents see the difference in their children and in their family life once the congregation has equipped the home with tools that nurture the Christian faith. A couple key questions remain: How many of the parents in our congregations still feel like they are "winging it"? How many feel like they are being equipped by their congregations? At least some parents notice the difference in the lives of their own children when they, the parents, are equipped and no longer winging it. The younger children in this example express curiosity, ask questions, and present an openness in their lives, the kind of daily life wonderment the church dreams of for its children of all ages.

Because of our recent history in American society where family life too often is considered antiquated and sometimes even harmful, we miss the excitement, openness, and eagerness that is present on the part of at least some parents. Clearly, it does no good to imagine every parent is eager and willing, but neither is it helpful or accurate to assume the opposite. Andrea Fieldhouse, director of family ministry and TYFI associate, expressed her delight in the eagerness of the parents she works with in a congregational educational program that helps parents teach and live the faith in the home. This director of family ministry states, "I think the key to this ministry is, you gotta want it and you gotta believe this is the way!" Referring to the families she works with she writes, "Parents are chomping at the bit for more knowledge about God and ways to have and raise faithful children. We make [parents] promise lots of important things at baptism and then we don't help them do it! They just simply don't know how, and certainly don't feel safe. Our job is to model, encourage, equip, hold their hand, affirm and help them practice faith!!!"[7] This director understands that most parents are not engaged in their role as primary teachers, guides, and models for the Christian faith, but some certainly want to be.

It is rather startling how forthcoming parents can be once they discover the possibilities for their important role and understand that the church is not there to be accusatory. One group of parents had a presentation from TYFI about their important role in the life of their children and other children as well. It was acknowledged that the church has not done a good job of supporting them as Christian parents, but their congregation was in the process of turning that around. The next day the Institute received an e-mail from one of the mothers present at the parenting class the night before. She began her comments with a confessional spirit:

*I'm not even sure where to start, so please bear with me.
This is very hard for me to do, but I feel that I owe it to my*

kids to do what I can. The discussions we had last night hit very close to home with me. It made me realize that I have failed my kids as far as helping them with their faith. I grew up in [the congregation] and went through Sunday school and confirmation and thought I did my part. I went away to college and lost touch with the church. Then when I was twenty my mother died of cervical cancer. I was so angry with God that you can't even imagine. At that time I turned my back on God and have not been able to find my way back to the church. . . So I thought I was doing right by my kids as long as I got them to Sunday school and Confirmation. I now realize how very wrong I was. I hope all of this doesn't sound like I've flipped my lid. I have made great changes in my life and want to find my way back to God. I just don't know how to go about it. I want to be able to be an example for my kids and help them to have a relationship with God. Can you help me?

This mother's candor far exceeds what we expect to hear from parents on a daily basis. True, there are many, many parents not ready for this kind of confession or this kind of pleading or commitment. But how many are there out there who would make similar confessions and commitments if only given the opportunity from a congregation ready to make a similar confession (that the congregation and larger church have not been as supportive of parents as it could be) and commitment (that the congregation is dedicated to support and equip parents and all adults grow in the grace of God for the sake of the reign of God and the needs of the world that God loves so completely in Christ)?

> Many parents are not engaged in their role as primary teachers, guides, and models for the Christian faith, but some certainly want to be.

And Grandparents

It is not only parents but grandparents and grandchildren who are ready to try to let their homes and their relationships be a source of faith nurturing powers. Pastor Greg Williams of Grace Lutheran Church in Hendersonville, North Carolina, described a Sunday where several youth were confirmed. The youth were asked to select a favorite passage from the Bible. In a conversation with the pastor prior to their confirmation that Sunday, these youth had talked to him about why that passage was important to them. That passage was then recited by the youth as part of the confirmation worship service. During the sermon, the pastor shared some of his meaningful Bible passages. The pastor concluded by inviting the worshipers to share and discuss passages over lunch that were especially meaningful to them. If they dined alone, they were encouraged to call or e-mail their children, nieces, nephews, grandchildren, or someone else and share their Bible passages and stories.

The following week, one couple told the pastor that they had, in fact, done what he had asked them to do. They had e-mailed their grandchildren and asked the grandchildren, in turn, to share their favorite Scripture passage and why it was meaningful. Within an hour that Sunday afternoon, they had replies from all but two. Before the evening ended, those last two had also responded.

One congregation had hosted a Hand in Hand congregational training event. After the Saturday Hand in Hand seminar, one couple went home and used some of the Four Key practices from that day. They had their two grandchildren over for the weekend. When the children went to bed that night, the grandparents blessed each of them with words and by making the sign of the cross on their foreheads. After blessing the younger child and then the older child, the younger responded, "Grandpa and Grandma, can you do that again?" Both grandparents were touched. The next day after worship, the grandparents took the grandchildren out to lunch, a rather typical activity for the foursome. However, this time when the four were at the restaurant, the grandparents got out FaithTalk® with Children[8] cards, a resource they had purchased at the Saturday seminar, and began having conversations about faith for an extended period of time. These combined activities over Saturday evening to Sunday morning seemed so inspiring and encouraging to the grandparents that Sunday evening they wrote down the whole story for the pastor, thanking him for hosting the weekend event and noting how it had already impacted their own lives, especially as grandparents.

These testimonials are not intended to indicate this as the norm for our homes, at least not yet. Most parents, grandparents, and other mentors have not even imagined the possibilities, dreamed such dreams, or hoped such hopes. These stories simply suggest that with some encouragement, enthusiasm, and training, people can feel equipped enough to try something, and little steps can make a big difference. Change happens when and where people are ready or willing to take the plunge (or even take a few steps into the shallow end of the water). Who knows who will respond, but if the seed is not cast, how can any faith nurturing take root and grow? With all the soccer-moms, Little League dads, piano-practicing kids, and who-knows-what other activities with chauffeuring parents and other adults leading the way, just wonder how many adults and kids may be ready to take a time out for a morsel of porridge that feels and tastes more like experiences that celebrate life instead of exhausting schedules, meals on the run, and precious little time to capture what is, in fact, precious.

Mission Statements for the Home

It has been a few decades now since congregations have incorporated mission statements, especially shorter ones that can be recited by the community. It has become an important way for everyone associated with the ministry of the congregation to understand and join the mission. Mission statements have developed into a strategic way to move beyond the congregation as a social community for insiders and toward a community of faith for the priesthood of all believers. Perhaps it is time for each congregation to lift up the mini-congregations in its midst, homes that are also an expression of the church and that include one or more apostle, bishop, and priest in each dwelling. One way to lift up and value mentors, aunts and uncles, grandparents, parents, and other church leadership in the home is the development of family mission statements. This way, parents and children, young adults and older adults could envision more clearly the critical role they play in celebrating, serving, and growing in a vital Christian faith.

A family mission statement or a mission statement for the home can honor and promote the priesthood of all believers who live and work and hope and pray with one another daily. It serves as a way to acknowledge the spiritual life of the home.[9] Each home can be lifted up as a place to experience the presence of God in the midst of love and celebrations as well as heartache and despair. In homes with small children, a family mission statement can remind adults to be aware of the sense of mystery in children's lives. As Martin Marty recently pointed out, for too long we have approached children as a problem to be solved instead of a mystery to welcome and enjoy.[10] It is in the awareness of mystery that we are open to the divine.

The very process of developing a family mission statement or a mission statement for one's home life can be an exercise in edifying the faith that binds people together in the mystery of God's love and a life in Christ. Here are three examples of mission statements for the home:

> *Our/My home is dedicated to loving God and neighbor through caring conversations, devotions, service, and rituals and traditions.*

> *Baptized in the name of the Triune God, the (name) family seeks to follow Jesus, caring for one another, friend, family, church, and world through God's word that guides us in faith, hope, and love.*

> *We seek to welcome all others as God has welcomed us that we may celebrate, serve, and grow in Christ's grace, mercy, and peace.*

The home can be enjoyed as an expression of the church, a place to learn, to serve, and to wonder about and question the deeper issues of life like birth and death and the meaning of both. The home can be esteemed as a place to receive and to give, to play and pray, to welcome in family and stranger alike, and, by the grace and power of God, to discover from the eyes and ears and voices of multiple generations what is honorable, just, pure, pleasing, commendable, excellent, and worthy of praise (see Philippians 4:8). One's home life represents a cherished setting where people can practice caring conversations, a devotional life, service for others and creation, and rituals and traditions that call people back to who and whose they are. The home is the perfect place to emphasize Christian hospitality, the kind that welcomes in family, friend, and stranger, the kind that expresses faith, hope, and love with words, deeds, and imagination filled with grace, mercy, and peace. Mission statements for homes and not just congregations can be a worthwhile means of honoring children and adults, mothers and fathers, grandparents, godparents, siblings, mentors, friends, and friends yet to be made as God-given gifts for a life of faith and service.

And the congregation serves as the intended place to lift up the home and daily life with this vision of being the church, with a spirit of respect, awe, and reverence for the work of God in one's dwelling and everyday relationships. The congregation is the logical place and community that provides the resources to facilitate experiences and a passion for the home as church, too. Every time people gather, the congregation becomes an opportunity for congregational servant-leaders to equip the home with this vision and with the encouragement, practices, and resources to be the church in and through the home to fill all of one's daily life. Worship and preaching can actively and consciously offer examples and samples of the Four Keys to take home.[11] Faith formation opportunities like baptisms, Bible studies, and mission trips need to be brought home for further consumption in small groups or for individuals. All that happens in the life of the congregation can and needs to be understood as dress rehearsal for the living of the word of God in one's life moment by moment, day by day.

The mission of the congregation is to be complemented by the mission into and out of the front door of the homes connected with the congregation. The prayers and hymns of worship become the nighttime prayers and table graces of the home. The sermon does not end with the "amen" but continues in the thoughts and conversations it stimulates. The service activities on behalf of the neighbor and creation promoted by the congregation become the lived experience and commitments of family and friends throughout the week. The gestures of kindness and faith, the blessings extended, the faithful routines of prayers, Scripture reading and more, the celebrations and memorials, the visuals created and received—all the Christian practices that one can imagine and experience in the congregation are to be brought home and relived again and again and again. All that happens in and through the congregation at the same time blesses, equips, and honors the church lived in and through the home.

> " Church in the home addresses much more than parents with children living under one roof. "

Not Just Parents

This chapter has given close attention to the importance of thoughtfully, gracefully, and faithfully honoring the life of the home and encouraging congregational leaders to see how families do want their homes to be a place of love and faith. Implicit in this is the need to support and equip parents in their God-given task of raising children, youth, and adults as people of faith, people who serve, people who hope, value, and believe what only the reign of God can bring.

At the same time, every adult serves the role of parent. A Christian ethical position maintains that all Christian adults are Christian parents. Therefore, it is important to read this chapter with others in mind besides parents with children in the home. The chapter refers to other caregivers, including grandparents, godparents, uncles, aunts, neighbors, teachers, coaches, employers, coworkers, and many, many others. These roles, too, are worthy to be esteemed and equipped for ministry with and on behalf of children, youth, and all others. For example, not many godparents feel confident about what they are to do and how they are to connect with godchildren as faith mentors. A few tips and resources from the congregation (for example, giving a homemade baptismal birthday card or an age-appropriate devotional book, doing some act of community service together, or even offering a table grace when the godparent and godchild are together) can go a long way. The encouragement, ideas, and resources can give godparents confidence and help them engage with their godchildren in a way that serves as a powerful witness to the Christian faith. In this way, the faith of both the godchild and godparent is nurtured.

Hopefully, it is now abundantly clear that the church in the home addresses much more than parents with children living under one roof. The spirit of understanding and mercy is for parents and all other caregivers, all other disciples of Christ. To be sure, parents need an extra dose of respect and support, but so does the single adult whose life is also a model and guide to others, so too the godparent, the probation officer, and the waitress, all of whom are caring for God's children. Once the Great Omission is named and addressed, the entirety of a congregation's ministry is redefined. No longer does it become the place to do the ministry of the church as much as it is the place to equip the larger church for a life of ministry.

A Final Word

As you continue to reflect on the Great Omission and how congregations and Christian homes can address it, step away from the culturally conditioned assumptions that parents and other adults don't care, won't engage, and can't do much anyway. See with fresh eyes, perceive with a renewed imagination, and wonder with the Scripture where the next Sarah and Abraham may be dwelling, the next Moses may be wandering, the next Deborah may be leading, the next Samuel may be sleeping, the next David may be shepherding, the next young maiden may be praying, the next fisherman may be waiting, the next Nathaniel may be skeptical but open, the next Martha may be serving, the next Mary may be listening, the next Zachaeus may be hiding, the next Samaritan woman at the well may be thirsting, the next Nicodemus may be questioning, the next Good Samaritan may be intervening, and the next unlikely candidate that may become the next grandparent, godparent, parent, in-law, mentor, or friend made ready to live a vibrant faith nurtured in daily life relationships and honored, supported, and equipped through the life of the congregation.

With great enthusiasm, a pastor recently forwarded an e-mail example of the unexpected ways in which a home has gladly embodied the life of the church. The pastor is from a congregation that has been coached in the Vibrant Faith Frame for two years. As an example of how the ministry is going there, he begins, "I ask you—how awesome are some of our folk?" He then goes on to explain that Diane is on church council and her daughter is getting married in June. He concludes his introduction of Diane's account by stating, "Just wanted to share a bit of what's cooking around here . . ."

Diane's Story

Diane begins her email to her pastor by noting that she wants to get a FaithChest for her daughter's wedding. She continues, I know how and where to go to get one. I want to use it during the wedding ceremony to place the unity candle on and also to hold a family Bible and some other mementos (maybe even their wedding album). Do you have a recommendation for a family Bible that they can use that has more modern language and also some resources for interpretation? Are there any other resources that you feel would be helpful for them?

This is a surprise, so don't say anything to [the name of the couple].

Once I get the Bible, I will have [groom's] parents mark up some favorite verses and David and I will do the same. I thought this would be a wonderful way for them to celebrate future anniversaries by lighting their unity candle and having a special renewal of their vows. If you can think of anything else that would be nice to include in the chest, we will put that in as well.

Thanks! Diane

With fresh, faith-filled, and optimistic eyes, continue to wonder where the next Diane and David will come from. How about from your congregation?

5

The Business of the Church

Recognizing the need for doing ministry with a fresh perspective and strategies is critical for the church of every age, including today. Identifying new ways of conceiving and engaging in ministry in homes, congregations, and communities is essential. However, effectively leading a faith community toward change that serves the vision and mission of the people of God is no easy task. Just ask Moses or any of the apostles! It is one thing to conceive; it is quite another to give birth.

Our congregational leaders need help during a time in history that most staff and lay leaders have not been trained to deal with. Translation of the challenge using multiple metaphors:

Shepherding a congregation includes numerous pitfalls, voracious wolves, and unanticipated challenges.

It is startling and disconcerting how one simple link in a chain can make the whole necklace fall apart.

Likewise, it is amazing how missing a hurdle can stop the running of a race (or how one person or committee or event can derail a congregation's momentum, at least for a time).

The more the church is aware of these pitfalls, weak links, or hurdles during this period of historic change, the more continuing education, workshops, congregational trainings, and coaching can become integral to today's church.

Leadership involves more than the office of pastor, but to be effective, it does include the role of pastor. It takes a faith village working together to nurture the Christian faith, and the pastor is in a pivotal role to help congregations and homes do just that. Only the pastor regularly preaches the word to the congregation. Only the pastor combines preaching, teaching, and administrative leadership with her or his particular vision and sense of mission.

> What is the business of the church if not the nurturing of Christian faith in the lives of the people served by the congregation?

Three Pastoral Types

At least three types of pastoral identity get in the way of effective leadership. The following three types or styles hinder serving the vision and mission of congregations seeking to move from the Great Omission to promote a vibrant faith in individuals, households, congregations, and communities. One is the pastor in a straightjacket; one is the Energizer Bunny pastor, and one is the pastor praying, blessing, and affirming from on high. All these leadership postures, these models of shepherding, create pitfalls, open the gates for wolves to enter, loosen links that hold ministry together, and trip on hurdles that leave ministry short of the finish line.

The Pastor in a Straightjacket

More than one pastor has experienced the discouraging reaction of an influential church council, board, or vestry member. The pastor steps into the monthly meeting excited to introduce or further present the Vibrant Faith Frame by guiding the leadership through a Four Key experience. Maybe it is presented through a devotional exercise or by structuring the entire meeting on the basis of caring conversations, devotions, service, and rituals and traditions. And then it happens. The pastor is interrupted and broadsided by a determined, self-confident, and established member on the council or board. "Pastor, I'm not interested in a Bible study or to sit here and chat with my friends. I can do that anytime. I am here to do the business of the church." The pastor is sufficiently intimidated, flustered, and silenced. The Four Key presentation may continue that evening, but it is quite possible that it will not be reintroduced the next month.

What is the business of the church if not the nurturing of Christian faith in the lives of the people served by the congregation? The pastor who just attempted to introduce the Four Keys into the lifeblood of the congregation for the sake of promoting a vibrant faith in people's lives was likely challenged by the fear of change, the fear of the unknown, and perhaps the fear of a real and living God. As Bill Easum articulated so well, the sacred cow of the church is control.[1] It is the behavior that can infest congregational boards and stifle the work of the Spirit in the life of the people of God.

The voice of control heard in some congregational leadership teams works to stifle innovation, to prevent faithful trial-and-error attempts at following God's cloud by day and fire by night—the experience of Moses and the people of the exodus out of Egypt. During the time of the exodus, the people grumbled at Moses and spoke as though they preferred the slavery and persecution in Egypt to facing the unknowns of the journey into freedom. (The contrast between the work of God as benefactor and the people's continued grumblings are dramatically evidenced in numerous accounts, including Exodus 15-17 and Numbers 21:1-9.). All the people wanted was to stay alive, no matter what the cost, even if life was slavery and persecution. On that front, not much has changed over thousands of years.

The voice of control, the voice that says, "I'm here for the business of the church," is often well intentioned and well meaning. That person has "seen it all before" without fruitful results. That voice is discouraged; it is not necessarily seeking to be unfaithful to the mission of the church. Yes, it is true, the motivation can be more toxic than well intentioned, but it need not be so to create deadly outcomes.

What does motivate many congregational boards? At conferences and congregational trainings, I have playfully reported data from my own imaginary Anderson Research Associates, Inc. The study is the motivation for evangelism exemplified by congregational councils, boards, and vestries. In this imaginary research project, leaders can give up to three answers as to why they are motivated to focus on the evangelism of the church. The conclusions (imaginary and playful, remember) are as follows:

Motivation for Evangelism Expressed by Some Councils, Boards, and Vestries

78%	Annual budget
65%	Fill empty pews
43%	Keep up with the non-denominational congregation down the street
27%	Comply with synod/district/diocesan goals
9%	For the love of God in Christ Jesus

To make it clear that this is "soft" research, I give it a margin of error of plus or minus thirty points. Clearly the "data" is intended to over-state the case to make a point. However, there is a way to verify data by comparing it to other data and by asking the "polled population" (the conference participants) how accurate the information seems to be. The attentive audiences that have reviewed this research provide overwhelming agreement with their nods and hesitant laughter. In fact, before the data is given to the group, people shout out that the number-one response for congregational motivation to evangelism is money. The other answers are given general assent.

Based on this "research" and the reaction to it, people in the church agree that the motivation for evangelism, one might call this the larger ministry of the church, can too often be equated with survival: keeping the doors open and the bills paid. That vision for congregational ministry stands in stark contrast with the historic faith of the Scriptures in the Risen Lord sending his followers out in the world, to "[g]o therefore and make disciples" (Matthew 28:19) and to do so not just in one's own congregation but "to the ends of the earth" (Acts 2:8). For some congregational leaders, the Christian faith of two thousand years has been substituted by a more conventional cultural religion that centers on personal comfort and safety and the distrust of outsiders, including the most recent pastor. The language of cultural religion is control, fear of something new, and "Pastor, I'm not interested in a Bible study." Cultural religion often leaves the pastor in a straightjacket.

The Energizer Bunny Pastor

This is the pastor most wanted by congregations, at least for a time. This pastor enters the congregation excited and ready for action. The pastor has just come from another congregation and knows much has been learned in the former setting that can now be applied to the new. Or the pastor has just finished a seminary degree or attended the latest and greatest seminar or continuing education program. No matter what the context, the pastor is enthusiastic and ready to work with a congregation that obviously wants the same things. Or maybe not.

One parishioner who deeply appreciates his Energizer Bunny Pastor describes the pastor's strengths as follows:

> *His organizational skills are excellent. He also has strong visionary ideas for our church's future. He is also very passionate about outreach. He wants all people to know our Lord and Savior. He wants everyone to feel comfortable in sharing this with our neighbors. He is a very caring pastor that would like more time to minister individually to people. Our family has met with him as a counselor and he is a great listener. Pastor gave us great spiritual guidance. He does an excellent job of preaching God's word. His sermons are very biblically sound and are able to incorporate Jesus into our everyday lives.*

The pastor appears to be that rare and gifted shepherd desired by most every congregation. When asked to state the pastor's work areas that could make his ministry stronger, this same person hesitates.

There is obvious deep respect for this pastor, but the respondent does begin to note the downside of unrestrained leadership,

> *I've no indications that there are any areas to work on. I would say that being too organized is a problem for some in our congregation. He is a focused individual with strong work ethics. Not all people understand, and I can appreciate that it could lead to disquietude. He is a strong advocate of setting goals. This is great for task-driven members, but this may be uncomfortable for some.*

Yes, the strong work ethic combined with a clear focus and goals will create great admiration by some and resistance, discomfort, and distrust from others. With an Energizer Bunny Pastor, rightly or wrongly, some will wonder about the genuineness of the pastor's motivation. As another parishioner observed, "Because of his boldness, sometimes that works against him in the fact that he is too quick to solve issues or 'push' new ideas on to people who are not ready. [He] sometimes comes off as manipulative."

Another respondent suggested that this same pastor "show support of all ministry areas, not just the ones that he is passionate about. To let go of the idea that things have to go exactly as he had planned." A challenge to being an Energizer Bunny Pastor is that even a highly motivated pastor has difficulty being an equal-opportunity cheerleader for all areas of ministry. Some who support areas of ministry not the target of the pastor may feel left out. The respondent also correctly suggests that others may have ideas and strategies worth attention.

After a while, the Energizer Bunny Pastor's energy creates resistance as well as support and enthusiasm. Some question the pastor's motives. The frustrations eventually move to conflicting perspectives in the congregation and a new pastoral vacancy. Some in the congregation will say it was due to a pastor who did not listen to or care for them. The pastor will say it was because it was the wrong call. The people wanted a family chaplain. The pastor wanted to do faithful ministry. Both voices may have missed a deeper truth.

The church can definitely benefit from the Energizer Bunny Pastor, as long as that pastor's energies and vision are tempered by much listening to others, learning from others, and pacing one's leadership at a rate that is sustainable for the larger congregational community. The ability to bring others on board with a clear vision and mission represents sound leadership, especially when the pastor is also able to incorporate the wisdom, vision, and mission others believe is their God-given ministry. Leadership is a two-way street. It utilizes the adage, "People support what they help create." No one person has all the wisdom from God in his or her own head. The church represents the entire body of Christ, not just a few pristine, ordained brain cells.

Praying, Blessing, and Affirming from On High Pastor

Then there is the pastor not straightjacketed or leading at lightning speed. This pastor seeks to preach the word in truth, lead worship according to established expectations, and generally let others do the leading. In some ways this seems good. Preach the word and let the Spirit guide the leadership of the community. The problem is, pastors are central to the leadership and activity of the congregation. One only needs to look at the pastoral wisdom shared by the Apostle Paul in the New Testament to see how concrete spiritual leadership gets.

Two Christian educators from a particular congregation came to a TYFI conference on a congregational faith formation strategy called Milestones Ministry. They came blessed with the support of their two pastors. These educators were adamant that the pastors were fully supportive of their efforts to implement the Four Keys through Milestones Ministry. The two were asked if either of the pastors had attended the recent TYFI conference in their area that taught the practices and principles. Neither had. The two were asked how either pastor was informed by or leading with these concepts. No examples could be given. By the end of the week, it was clear to these two Christian educators that they were given a nearly impossible assignment. If the pastor or pastors are not preaching, teaching, and leading with the practices and principles, how can others effectively guide the congregation to them?

Exemplary Congregations in Youth Ministry research concludes that effective ministry with and to youth (and effective congregational ministry generally) identifies the pastor as pivotal to the larger ministry of the congregation.[2] Effective youth ministry requires sound theology announcing God's gracious presence in the community and an understanding of church that brings the generations together to shape lives in Christ. The pastor is central to both of those tasks. Effective youth ministry does not begin with programs. The vision cast, the theology taught and preached, and the ministry of presence embodied by the pastor is essential. Praying for, blessing, and affirming the work and leadership of others is still important, but the pastor has to get his or her feet wet in the same ministry waters to be the ministry of the larger congregation, not simply the passion of a few.

One Christian educator working with children and their families knows of the limitations of having ministry assignments passed on to her without the active support and articulated vision of the pastors. She writes,

> If the pastor doesn't get it, you end up with just one more children's program. . .just for children. It's not thought of as a way of life and thus not supported in worship or any other ministry. Eventually it is just one more program that stops when the child reaches middle school. If it is supported by the pastor, then it carries the passion of the "office" of pastor with it, and to the congregation it becomes more valid and supported. Once the "powers that be" get it, it tends to permeate through the rest of the congregational family. I think that the pastors believe that what I have to say and share is important, true and probably vital, but to live it themselves. . .not so much.
>
> People like what they know, even if it doesn't work or the evidence shows that the church is dying and children are growing up without faith. . . . And so our pastors keep spinning their wheels, doing the same things that have always been done

and wondering why they aren't getting different results! And thus our children and families look other places for meaning and agendas. . .which the world is so delighted to offer.

The frustration on the part of this Christian educator is obvious. She has the passive support from her pastors that exists without passion or deeper appreciation of the centrality of the mission. Without that, her ministry stops at a certain age. Her ministry is siloed, cut off from the larger ministry of the whole. Pastors who pray, bless, and affirm from on high—or from a distance—do not shape the ministry of the whole congregation. People end up doing a little bit of this, a little bit of that, and nothing holds together with a seamless, lifelong faith.

" Effective youth ministry does not begin with programs. *"*

What's a Pastor to Do?

One bishop said it well: "The most frequent phone calls of complaint I get is about the pastors who don't lead. The second most complaints come from people who say their pastor leads too much." In a historic time like our own, when the conventional work of congregations seems to be working less and less effectively, pastors need to raise the clarion call to prayerfully and humbly dare to help lead the way. When it is time for the church to be on the move, leaders need to focus on following God's cloud by day and God's fire by night. But how?

Care-Giving and Direction vs. Micromanaging

To be pastors that lead—working with a team of others and seeking to follow God's lead by day (follow the cloud) and by night (the fire), they need to be both spiritual caregivers and organizational directors on behalf of the other leaders in the congregation. Unfortunately, pastors rarely see themselves in both those roles. If a pastor is not running five miles ahead of the congregation leading the distant charge (the Energizer Bunny), he or she is often not running at all (straight-jacketed or affirming from on high). In the latter case, the pastors don't want to meddle or micromanage the congregation's ministry. The belief is that God has blessed people with spiritual gifts that need to be honored, so the pastor trusts the hand of God at play in the congregation. The problem is that even God-gifted leaders need support and the various gifts do, like talented musicians in an orchestra, need to be brought together to play the same piece of music.

Pastors need to use their skills, training, and education as spiritual directors and organizational directors to care for and guide congregational leadership into the Vibrant Faith Frame. The pastor needs to give close attention and care to the lives of the other leaders. How is the Vibrant Faith Frame being lived in the lives of staff? Of council members? Of others who help lead in the life of the congregation? How can the gospel message be a comfort and a guide for the masses in the congregation if it is not so for the leaders who are teaching and endorsing it?

> " Congregational leaders need to be in touch with one another. "

Pastors and Other Leaders as Spiritual Caregivers

Over the years, large numbers of individual staff members and appointed lay leaders in congregations have been interviewed by TYFI. At times those congregations are recognized internally and in the larger community as quite successful. These are congregations doing marvelous things. And yet, the sense of satisfaction and delight has not necessarily touched the lives of the staff or other leaders. If that disconnect is not addressed, those successful congregations will eventually collapse like a house of cards.

Some staff members have expressed their deep grief, even to the point of tears, describing how difficult it is to do one program after another or one event after another that always has to be better than the last. Those were the implicit expectations, often reinforced by a pat on the back and word of approval for the latest attempts. Others have stated that they work with and for a wonderful pastor, but a person who is not a pastor to them. "The pastor has no idea what is going on in my life."

One associate pastor observed, "For seventeen years I had been the associate pastor under the same senior. Day in and day out he would pass me in the halls and I would wonder if he had any idea of what I was doing in the congregation or what was happening in my life." It is true that God blesses faith communities with the necessary gifts to do ministry in homes, congregations, and communities. As Paul wrote in 1 Corinthians, "You are not lacking in any spiritual gifts as you wait for the revealing of our Lord Jesus Christ" (1:7). But simply having various spiritual gifts available is not enough. Those gifts need to be implemented for the common good as one whole body. One of those gifts is for pastoral leadership and other congregational leaders to check in with the fellow ministers of the gospel on their own faith journey and understanding of their ministries (the role of spiritual caregiver) and to orchestrate the God-given gifts into a functioning and clear ministry (the role of organizational director). The associate pastor quoted here could have used both from his own colleague and senior pastor.

To move forward with a Christian ministry that has integrity, it has to be real for the people leading and teaching the ministry. For that to happen, the congregational leaders, including pastors, need to be in touch with one another. Are the Four Keys a part of their own lives? Where are the struggles? Where are the joys? What is getting in the way of meaningful lives and ministry? What is needed to help the leaders lead? What is going well that needs to be communicated to others with a spirit of encouragement to all? To ask those questions and to hear the responses, spiritual care is needed, not just measurable goals and performance appraisals. It is not micromanaging to care about what is going on in the lives and families of the people who serve in congregations. The operative term is not unwanted control or nosiness but interest, care, and a wise, listening, attentive soul. The implementation of the Vibrant Faith Frame will rarely happen without it.

It is worth noting that the Key of devotions is central to the spiritual care offered by the pastor, not only the personal devotions of the pastor but also the larger devotional life with fellow leaders. The faithful and prudent use of Scripture and prayer with others (in public worship as well as in a pastor's office), for example, touches on all of the Four Key faith practices. To pray with and for a partner in ministry suggests prior caring conversation that has given attention to the needs, joys, and pains of the other. To link another person's life to the work and will of God through Scripture and prayer serves the other with deep meaning and hope for a life lived well, at least by the standards of the cross. To take time for Scripture and prayer with another is a Christian tradition well worth planting in the middle of the congregation's ministry soil. Without such roots well planted, so much ministry can end up feeling like just another high-pressure job that rewards the survival of the fittest instead of the joy of the Christian journey faithfully followed.

> The spiritual caregiver leads on the basis of the reign of God, a vision of life dictated by the cross of Christ.

From a Fear of Micromanaging to Directing Vibrant Faith

In today's church culture, a strong tendency to avoid micromanaging exists. Of course, good leadership trusts the gifts and talents of others and should not be looking over the shoulders of others, but there needs to be more than a "hands off" attitude on the part of the leadership. The challenge is to envision a leadership style that moves beyond the fear of micromanaging yet without controlling everything that happens. While trusting the integrity and giftedness of others, those gifts still need to be used for the common good (1 Corinthians 12:7) as part of a larger whole. The alternative recommended here offers leadership that invests in the lives of those doing ministry (spiritual caregiver) and helps clarify, inspire, and coordinate the efforts to put together a clear and effective ministry (organizational director).

The role of spiritual caregiver helps people name and claim their gifts and address issues that get in the way of using those gifts. The spiritual caregiver leads on the basis of the reign of God, a vision of life dictated by the cross of Christ. The organizational director, like an orchestra director, prayerfully and faithfully embraces the piece that is to be played and makes sure that the musical talents of the orchestra members result in a clear and harmonious whole. Another image for this work is that of the project director. That person also deeply understands the talents of his or her team and knows what outcomes are needed. When the project is launched, it is due to the efforts of individuals brought into a team that delivers the desired product or service. Caring for and grooming individual lives of faith (spiritual caregiver) and bringing numerous lives and gifts together to arrive at the desired results (orchestra director or project director) represents the congregational leadership needed. Of course, all of the gifts of leadership are understood through the lens of humbly and expectantly following the lead of the Triune God.

One congregational pastor who is being coached to lead the Vibrant Faith Frame describes his thoughtful journey from avoiding micromanagement to leadership that provides spiritual care-giving and organizational direction as follows:

> As a lead pastor of capable lay professionals and support staff, I have assumed that they know what their responsibilities are and will carry them out without much need of my time. Staff meetings tend to the tasks and coordinate the schedules. Beyond the staff meeting, I get on with "my" particular tasks, assuming then that the staff will "automatically" do what they have to do and in this way make my life much easier. And for the most part that is what happens. I am grateful that we get along, like each other, and even have fun as we serve. We

function pretty well together. But I wonder if the way we relate to one another, the congregation, and our work is grounded in the very mission we are called to serve. In other words, as a community within a community of faith, do we tend to matters of faith? Or do we get overly focused on the tasks at hand and the need of the programs? And is my work with them a ministry, nurturing them in their understanding and practices of the faith?

I am learning that caring for the staff is indispensable in my care for the ministry of the whole. Listening to their stories, celebrating the unfolding gift of God's grace in their lives, and encouraging their gifts to flourish are truly my service to the gospel. Tending to staffing relationships fosters a healthy mutuality among all of God's people in our calling and mission. Now, I admit that such an approach calls for a new awareness on my part. . . . As I live out of a strong partnership in the gospel with my staff, the staff in turn is equipped to partner their gifts with the gifts of the congregation. For sure this means learning to trust and journey alongside the staff, taking their gifts and calling as seriously as all others.

This is the voice of a pastor making the transition from one who simply resisted micromanaging (staff members will carry out their responsibilities on their own) to one who is willing to claim his role as spiritual caregiver ("Is my work with them a ministry, nurturing them in their understanding and practices of the faith?"). He questions his style of pastoral leadership. He has been delighted to work with capable people so that he can do his work in other areas. Now he understands that their lives are part of his care and pastoral leadership. He understands the relational nature of faith formation that touches individual lives and through those lives touches others. He also recognizes the relational dimension of Christian ministry, the first of the Five Principles.

As this pastor connects more intentionally with his staff (and the non-paid leadership as well), he will have opportunities to orchestrate and direct the ministry into a larger whole. Many pastors assume that if the congregation has a mission statement and the other leadership is directed by the mission statement, then all efforts will lead in the same direction. However, that is not necessarily the case. People can and do interpret the same mission statements a bit differently or with a different emphasis. More intentional connections with others on staff and other non-paid elected and appointed leaders in the congregation will promote more efficient efforts and more satisfying results.

Pastor Tim Glenham from Morning Star Lutheran Church in Matthews, North Carolina, is another individual who has more fully grounded his pastoral identity in the role of spiritual caregiver as well as organizational leader (see the description of Morning Star council members giving their faith stories at council meetings and to the larger congregation in chapter 1, pp. 20–22). This development in pastoral identity has changed how he participates in church council meetings. For example, he no longer sees the opening devotion as a "rubber stamp" to begin the meeting. He sees council devotions as a way to equip council members to explore and deepen their own faith lives.

Pastor Glenham sees council members more and more as partners in ministry through their own spiritual journeys as they examine elements of the Vibrant Faith Frame. Now council devotions are a time for council members to discuss in small groups of two or three how the Four Keys guide their faith lives. He uses Taking Faith Home, a weekly resource used as a bulletin insert that Four Keys the lectionary Scripture texts used each Sunday. Council members use the resource for faith talk conversations, prayer time, service to each other and the congregation, and as a tradition that grounds the meetings in Christian ministry rather than agendas, power plays, and votes. Pastor Glenham then asks for one or two council members to talk about how the Four Keys have been part of their lives during the past month. Some of those stories are written up and used in the congregation's newsletter so that others can benefit from the experiences of their council leadership. What a wonderful idea! Here is one of those articles written by a council member:

On October 24 Wanda and I attended the rehearsal dinner of my niece Courtney and her fiancé Lin. The reason we were attending was we had asked if we could pass on our faith with a blessing. Courtney is the niece we shared a blessing of the faith with after her graduation from Lenoir-Rhyne a year ago.

In this blessing of the marriage, we presented the couple with a "cup of blessings." We had their initials engraved with 10/25/2008 on one side and "cup of blessings" on the other side of the goblet. We explained to all in attendance that we are filling the cup with wine (in this case it was grape juice by request) and we would pass the cup around for those who wish, including children, to fill the cup with a verbal blessing.

There were over forty people at the dinner and every person filled the cup with a blessing. The youngest there was my three-year-old great-nephew, and when he took the cup and said "God bless you," well, you can imagine what Wanda and my eyes did. That is what sharing and passing on the faith is all about. When the cup came back around to me, I told Courtney and Lin as all blessings come from God we must accept them and that by drinking from this cup you are accepting these blessings from your friends and family, but especially from God. We need to take the opportunities that come along to pass them on through our faith to our loved ones.

At the end of the evening Courtney came up and said "you guys do the best things for me." She asked where she could get a copy of the book we use, For Everything There Is a Season— 75 Blessings For Daily Life.[3] Guess what she's getting as a wedding present.

The Scripture for the blessing came from Philippians 2:1-4 and Genesis 12:2. Our prayer is for our family to see our faith in us and will then pass it on in their own families.

Here is an example of a pastor encouraging council leaders to live their Christian faith through the lens of the Four Keys and the Five Principles so that their Christian discipleship can more fully embody the attributes of being authentic, available, and affirming. It is all evident in the council member's story included above. Pastor Glenham is encouraging and guiding—in the language of today one might say, "coaching"—others in his congregation to explore, experience, and communicate their life in Christ. Is this not the pastoral leadership needed by the church, pastors and others who shepherd the lives of Christians to live their lives more fully in the context of the life of Christ?

Not only does Pastor Glenham's leadership embody spiritual care giving, it also exemplifies sound organizational leadership. The council member's story is retold not only at the council meeting but also through the newsletter, so that other lives can be touched and encouraged by the story. A valuable piece of organizational leadership is to encourage the larger body to reflect actively upon and use the vision endorsed by the congregation. Here the Vibrant Faith Frame is reinforced and restated as something that is actually happening in the lives of people in the congregation. This is a strategic way to get the vision and mission of the congregation to become more fully owned and practiced by the larger congregational community.

Some may object to this view of congregational leadership because spiritual care and directing the larger efforts of the congregation take time. However, the alternative of not attending to the spiritual care of others and orchestrating ministry will result in congregations spinning in circles where even more time is needed to address the pain and frustrations experienced within the life of the congregation as well as the homes of the members and friends of the congregation. An example of this is the feedback received by TYFI from congregations that structure council meetings based on the Four Keys (for example, including caring conversations at the beginning of the meeting, using devotions that focus on AAA discipleship, awareness that the meeting is intended as a service to neighbor in thanksgiving to God, and lighting a candle at the beginning of the meeting to remind the council members that the light of Christ is central to all they are and do). Instead of taking more time, the meetings begin to focus more quickly on what matters to the council members, and the meetings end up being shorter than before.

The role of spiritual caregiver and organizational director (that is, orchestra or project director) is not limited to the office of pastor. Once the pastor leads in this way, it becomes easier for others to follow suit. The goal in congregational ministry is not simply to get stuff done but to live and work together in such a way that lives are cared for and the desired ministries happen. Caring for the faith life of one another (spiritual care) is as important as the service offered on behalf of others (organizing ministries). This preferred style of leadership checks in with others to see how they are doing in their daily faith journey and how the intended ministries are working in the mission fields of homes, congregation, community, and larger world.

6

EFFECTIVE LEADERSHIP WITH THE VIBRANT FAITH FRAME

The challenge to effective leadership using the Vibrant Faith Frame is that the shift in thinking can be so subtle and the established church culture so pervasive that the relational dimension of faith formation can be overlooked without even realizing it. Another related challenge to the Vibrant Faith Frame is that some leaders have become so invested in keeping a local congregation's doors open that that goal becomes an end in itself. If there is enough income to keep the heat on and the doors open, then the work of the church is being served. With that thinking, expectations for the church and the kingdom of God on earth (a petition in the Lord's prayer) have been seriously compromised. In the midst of these and other challenges to any significant change in the life of a congregation, four tips may help leaders during the time of transition from the church of the Great Omission to the congregation of the Vibrant Faith Frame.

The first is language. Be clear about the language that is used. It presents a specific vision, assumptions, and goals. The second is patience. It took the church generations to become entrenched in the Great Omission. It will take time to give birth to another way of seeing, thinking, and doing ministry. The third is the awareness that creating a new habit demands more than just patiently holding on to a new vision with language, goals, and strategies. Helping individuals and homes establish new habits consistent with the Vibrant Faith Frame will take disciplined work to foster new ways of behaving as well as thinking. Finally, the Vibrant Faith Frame is about the Christian faith that is authentic, available, and affirming. That authentic, available, and affirming faith includes the human element of doubt. The reality of doubt needs to be named and honored as part of an authentic Christian experience. Without this admission, it will be difficult for authentic, humble, and at times humbled lives to dare to engage the journey of the Christian faith with any real seriousness and, more importantly, courage.

> An authentic, available, and affirming faith includes the human element of doubt.

Language Establishes Assumptions and Goals

The language we use reveals our priorities. More than one congregation has used language to communicate the goal of increased Sunday worship attendance or of getting more people "involved in church" without identifying the more necessary commitment to the work of Christian discipleship. The language used in such stated goals or desires says more about a concern for congregational survival than it does about faithfully following Jesus.

For example, after a year of coaching a congregation, I returned for an annual check-in with the congregation. Part of the experience of a coaching check-in is to hear the questions, ideas, excitement, and issues of the congregation as it has been focusing on the principles, practices, and strategies recommended by the Vibrant Faith Frame. In this particular instance, a meeting was held in the sanctuary immediately following a worship service. During the discussion that ensued, the congregational president began by identifying a primary agenda: "One of my concerns is how to get new members more involved." The language that conveyed his priority and primary goal was the two words "more involved." The concern identified a rather typical goal of congregational leaders: How do we get people to show up regularly to the congregation's facilities and programs? It is not that the concern is illegitimate, but it suggests that the congregational president was not focusing on the language, assumptions, and goals of correcting the Great Omission.

I acknowledged that the president's concern was legitimate on one level but was still limiting. The president's concern to get new members involved probably meant getting new members more involved in the life of the congregation. While involvement instead of being disengaged from the life of the congregation is an important concern, addressing that goal does not necessarily begin by enticing people to the sanctuary. The involvement of new members could mean being more involved in following Christ as a disciple in the world. It could mean being more involved in the church in the home of the new members. It could mean being more involved with others in the congregation and community in small group ministry in homes and in public, community settings.

I suggested that the idea of "involvement" be redefined and that each new member be invited to the home of an established (meaning "not new") member of the congregation. There the new member (or members from one or more households) would experience the vibrant faith of the congregational community through Christian hospitality and the use of the Four Key faith practices. I recommended that each new member or new member family be invited to three homes from the congregation during the first six months to experience the church culture promoted by the congregation, a church culture that lifted up and valued the grassroots faith life of homes and neighborhoods.

At the end of the evening, some people informed me that one of the long-standing members of the congregation had just walked up to a couple that had joined the congregation a few months before and invited them to his home for dinner.

A month later I asked for further feedback from the pastor regarding the evening event and my challenge to the president and congregation. The pastor noted that there were a few remarks like, "Well, Pastor, we still have to get them to come to church." The pastor also commented that the couple invited that evening was now developing a more personal relationship with the host family, a concrete example of becoming "more involved" in church if not exactly "at" church. The pastor also commented on the recent history of the congregation and their understandable anxiety about numbers after their "glory days of the 50s" when the congregation was bustling with people. He acknowledged that they are people who genuinely want to reach out to other people but for a number of reasons are currently a bit hesitant.

I confess that I too want those glory days back. I want congregations brimming with people but not just to fill pews and feel good about the appearance of the public church. I want those pews filled because people's lives are routinely being renewed by the gospel and they want to worship together, celebrate the faith in Christian fellowship, and be equipped to be the church every day and night in home, community, and world.

That is the understanding and approach taken by Paul Nelson, a pastor in Eden Prairie, Minnesota. His congregation is taking in approximately forty to fifty homes a year. The new member classes focus on how the gospel impacts their lives in their own homes and beyond their homes. He intentionally does not focus on what new members can do for the congregation. His conviction is that once people are supported in their daily life and faith, especially through the Four Keys, they will want to be a part of a Christian community that equips them for their daily discipleship. The new membership class teaches what it means to be the church through the Five Principles and how their lives are blessed to be a blessing through the Four Keys.

The commitment to getting more people involved "in church" represents language, assumptions, and goals associated with the church that one imagines. Without clear language, assumptions, and goals, the journey of being the church doesn't even feel worth taking. Clergy and other staff have described their ministries as lacking a clear direction: "I feel like I am spinning my wheels." Who wants to do that?

A Spirit of Patience and Understanding

It takes time for congregational leaders to see beyond the immediate anxieties of lower worship attendance. And it takes time to be fluent with a new language and the Christian life it represents. It is the premise of the Vibrant Faith Frame that when the congregation advocates for discipleship and evangelism as its primary mission, especially the kind of discipleship and evangelism that focuses on the faith life in homes and through cross+generational relationships outside the walls of the congregation, then over time worship attendance will, by the grace and mercy of God, once again be more robust. It is essential that the congregation's primary mission be grounded in a sense of biblical discipleship and evangelism that leads to a growing worship attendance, not simply public worship attendance that may or may not result in effective discipleship and evangelism.

The simple exercise of showing up for worship, Sunday school, or youth group does not fulfill the task of addressing people's lives with the word of God. For too long the standard of "success" for congregations was simply about numbers associated with a congregational event. Have the numbers in worship and study gone up or gone down? The scorecard for measuring the effectiveness of congregational ministry needs to expand beyond those limited numbers. Such a cultural shift in language, assumptions, and goals does take time. One year or two years of focusing on a revitalized vision and mission will not be enough time to overcome a lifetime of church culture that has given more attention to numerical assessments and survival than renewal.

One result of the impatience of congregational leaders—especially pastors passionate about Christian discipleship over against congregational membership and outreach into the world over maintaining a viable organization—is the inconsistency of the language used in the congregation. The glossary of terms tends to keep changing in these congregations. Some congregational leaders have described it as the "book of the month club" mentality. There are many contemporary books on congregational life and leadership. Enthusiastic pastors succumb to the temptation of overloading congregational leaders and worshippers with a rich variety of terms. This process confuses people and, quite often, the enthusiastic pastors as well. Staff and other leaders wonder where the congregation is headed next month or next year. As one key leader in a congregation put it, "I don't want to be changing the vision every eighteen months." The senior pastor of that congregation heard that message loud and clear and made amends to slow down the church leadership vocabulary tests.

It is of utmost importance for congregational renewal, including the renewing of the faith life of our homes, that congregational leadership identify and stick to a core glossary of terms that define and guide any other concepts that are introduced into the ministry of the congregation. The core concepts offer an umbrella under which all other strategies become interpreted and useful to the larger ministry of the congregation. What is not acceptable is to change the core language, the umbrella language, every year or two based on the latest and most popular book, author, or school of thinking regarding congregational life, discipleship, evangelism, or stewardship. The current era of congregational self-assessment, repentance, and renewal needs foundational terms that help individuals and congregations attend to Christian discipleship and outreach. Using purpose-driven language one year, then moving to a separate list of core discipleship terms proposed by a book or denomination another year, then to a congregational survey tool with its distinct language and vision, and then to the Vibrant Faith Frame does not allow the stability and clarity to help congregational leaders work effectively as a team.

Attentiveness to a vibrant Christian faith requires a common language so that people can communicate effectively with one another. If the congregation is going to do its ministry in English, then speak English. If in Spanish, then speak Spanish. Figuratively speaking, difficulties arise when the people start their ministry speaking one language like English, then have to learn Spanish the next year, and then try to learn to do ministry in Hebrew or Swahili. Just as a congregation needs to be fluent in a common language like English or Spanish to communicate effectively with each other, so too the congregation needs to be fluent in a visionary language to communicate with each other regarding its ministry, strategies, and outcomes.

The Vibrant Faith Frame offers foundational language that provides principles for being the church—a faith forming community—practices for living and maturing in the Christian faith, and a clear picture of the essential characteristics of a follower of Jesus. This does not mean that insights, language, and strategies cannot be added, but it does mean not losing the core, umbrella language that guides and defines all other concepts.

Undoubtedly, some reading this (especially pastors) are thinking, "but we have our language. It is grounded in our biblical and theological heritage." In fact, that is a point well taken. Each denomination's heritage (including the non-denominational denominations) already gives congregations a solid grounding with language that guides ministry. However, even that language is often corrupted by the twentieth-century, institutional culture. For example, a number of denominations use language like "means of grace" or "word and sacrament ministry" to direct their efforts in local congregations. Unfortunately, that language often has gone through reductionistic interpretations that limit the language to a Sunday morning event of standing in a pulpit, behind an altar, and beside a baptismal font or other water source. Of course the ministry includes those locations and voices of authority for the work of the Holy Spirit in the church. However, "means of grace" and "word and sacrament ministry" means more than an endorsement of the resident expert. It means more than a Sunday morning location and the office of pastor invested with the authority of the church. Other language is available within the various theological traditions that broaden the base of interpretation beyond a Sunday morning experience, like the "priesthood of all believers," and that language can benefit from an awareness and correction of the Great Omission.

For example, one congregational pastor nearing retirement reflected on his years in his current congregation. He served a congregation with a strong history and endorsement of word and sacrament ministry. He observed,

Ten years ago I would have said that the congregation had a bright future, but now I don't think so. People don't visit this place as often, and those who do don't stay as long. The parents say that their kids just don't want to come because it's not fun here for them. The kids want a youth group filled with activities and lots of other kids. Our niche just doesn't seem to draw new people. There are too many other congregations attracting people with bigger programs for children and youth.

This pastor has become discouraged and resigned to the idea that the congregation will experience a slow but inevitable death. It is a congregation with a rich history of quality preaching and worship but not a clear vision for evangelism and discipleship beyond the Sunday morning hour, a congregation that could benefit from language, assumptions, and goals set forth in the Vibrant Faith Frame.

This stands in clear contrast to a pastor who recently observed that people were coming and worshipping and staying in his congregation not simply because of programs but because of language, strategies, intentionality, and a welcoming presence offered by the Vibrant Faith Frame. He writes,

We are a thriving congregation in a growing retirement area. We are richly blessed with experienced disciples. We are striving to become thriving with younger disciples also.

As part of our strategic planning process and implementation, we hosted a Hand in Hand training for the congregation.[1] This initiated additional intentionality for ministries and hospitality aimed at children, youth, and younger families. Some ministries we implemented, including the following: Taking Faith Home Sunday handouts (bulletin inserts that give Four Key ideas every week to be practiced in the home); "Christian Parenting" Sunday school class; monthly Passing on Faith workshops for parents of younger children (a class that teaches the role of the home in faith formation); and utilizing the 5-4-3 language in publications and worship.

Several months into this, a member shared that on this particular Sunday, he and his wife—separately—had each introduced themselves and welcomed two different young families. They each asked, "What brought you to Grace?" Both said, "We came back and are planning to join because this place values children, and that's what we want." One even noted how they had visited other congregations with much larger children and youth ministries.

As pastor, my heart leaped within me to hear that already, early in this developing ministry, the Spirit was working and touching lives of parents who want the partnership of a church family in passing on faith in Jesus Christ to their children.

The contrast between these two pastors could not be more evident. The first pastor has resigned himself to discouragement and the impending closure of a congregation's doors and ministry. The other communicates excitement and delight at some initial responses to the use of the Vibrant Faith Frame (described above as the 5-4-3) that shaped language, ministry, and a welcoming and confident attitude within the congregation. Whereas the one pastor felt defeated by a sense of competition with congregations that offer larger programs for children and youth, the other pastor saw older members as "experienced disciples" who could be a meaningful part of child, youth, and family ministry and a vision that focused on discipleship and outreach. That vision encourages a congregational environment that equips the faith life of homes, an approach that interested visitors and even encouraged members to interview visitors on their reactions.

Both pastors and congregations represent the same denomination and theological heritage. The one pastor had given up. The other was patiently grooming congregational leaders with language and a vision that suggested what was happening in the life of the congregation was impacting lives and nurturing disciples through the word of God, the means of grace that was working in relationships and in homes as well as within the ministries of the congregation.

> Congregational leaders wanting renewal in their midst will want to help people create new ways of thinking and behaving.

Creating New Habits

Congregations that make a difference do not simply offer new language, assumptions, and goals. They support the formation of new habits, of a variety of everyday Christian practices, faith practices like those that flow out of the Four Keys. As one pastor noted, "Our congregation is great at getting resources into the home, but we have no idea if those resources are being used." Congregations must learn if those resources are being used (see the next chapter on doing research in the congregation), and when they are not, help people to implement the tools and establish new habits consistent with the Christian faith and life (as opposed to the habits consistent with consumer capitalism, a dominant religion in America).

In the past, congregational leaders have seen it as their job to offer worship, education, and Christian fellowship opportunities. The assumption was that what people did with those experiences was up to them. In other words, people came to the congregation, had a variety of experiences, and were sent out the door with the implied message, "Good luck; we hope this makes a difference for you." Wishful thinking is not good enough. Giving good ideas and tools are not good enough anymore. Congregational leaders need to give more attention to follow-up, discovering how the ministry of the congregation is impacting lives. When the intended renewal does not appear to be happening, then leaders need to slow down and help people create the new habits of nurturing the Christian faith in the home through the Four Keys.

The tendency in congregations is to offer ministry that is a mile wide and an inch deep. Congregations try lots of different activities to interest members but without any understanding of how any of it really leads to lives of Christian repentance and renewal. For the sake of congregational renewal, the kind that renews the life of faith of individuals and households, it is time for congregations to do fewer activities but go deeper with the ministries they do. Follow up initial faith-forming congregational events (for example, a program that teaches how to celebrate the Christmas season in the home) with other events that reinforce earlier faith forming gatherings (for example, a follow-up event that discusses what happened in the homes during the Christmas season). This is a way for congregations to research the lives of the people who participate in congregational activities and explore ways to help the people become more disciplined in their daily discipleship.

Attention to the importance of creating new habits will affect how congregations use their news media, like bulletins, newsletters, and websites. Instead of simply promoting future events, congregations will want to use more of their news media to review what has happened to reinforce how those congregational ministries impacted lives. Telling stories of how individuals and households were impacted by the ministries in the congregation will encourage others to see how lives are being formed by Christ and how their own lives can also be impacted by a life in Christ.

It is no longer enough to offer ideas and tools that reflect the Christian faith and life. Congregational leaders wanting renewal in their midst will want to help people create new ways of thinking and behaving. That means more than sitting in a pew for an hour a week. It reflects the practice of Christian repentance that leads people to "walk in newness of life" (Romans 6:4) and understand that they have been "created in Christ Jesus for good works, which God prepared beforehand to be our way of life" (Ephesians 2:10b). Without this attention to new habits and a new way of life, what will happen was described centuries ago by Martin Luther during the Reformation: "As a result they live like simple cattle or irrational pigs and, despite the fact that the gospel has returned, have mastered the fine art of misusing all their freedom."[2] Congregational leaders don't want that, do they?

" Biblical faith incorporates doubt into the life of faith. "

Real Doubt for Real Biblical Faith

Encouraging congregations, households, and individuals to lift up a vibrant faith that is authentic and that impacts individuals and communities alike is not meant to be understood as an easy assignment, like a paint-by-number picture. Faith is messy. Family life is messy. Congregational life is messy. And yet to be the church, the body of Christ, and to focus on supporting and nurturing the Christian faith means stepping into the swampy waters of all those messy realities: faith, family, congregation, and even the larger world beyond.

There appears to be a viewpoint presented in today's culture about religion that suggests that faith is simple, black and white, clear-cut, and very doable if only one brings a willing heart. Decide for Jesus and life will be easy. You will become rich; you will certainly experience a tranquil and peaceful heart. That may reflect the understandings of cultural religion but certainly not biblical, historic Christianity. The problem is that these cultural assumptions about faith have crept deeply into the fabric of congregational life. As a result, individuals find it quite difficult to talk about their own fears, doubts, and questions regarding Christianity in general and their own experience of faith in particular.

No effort to address the needs for a vibrant faith for individuals and for larger faith communities dare ignore this major hurdle: doubt. Fortunately, the cultural religion that promotes certainty is being challenged today, particularly by young adults and an emergent

church movement that understands that life and faith involve questions, ambiguities, complexities, and doubts that need to be acknowledged and taken with utmost seriousness.

"Jesus has a very special love for you. As for me, the silence and
the emptiness is so great that I look and do not see, listen and do not
hear."[3] These are the words of Mother Teresa to the Rev. Michael Van
Der Peet written in 1979. These and other very personal and confessional writings are part of an autobiographical book, *Mother Teresa:
Come Be My Light*, that reveals the "dark night" of faith that she, like
St. John of the Cross and many others before her, experienced. The
revelations have stunned a world familiar only with her public per-
sona, her work in Calcutta, and her Missionaries of Charity. This icon
of Christian faith suffered the deepest kind of doubt, not hearing or
seeing or sensing the presence of God in her life. Some consider this
the epitome of hypocrisy (a term she herself used about herself); others consider this the deepest example of true faith.

Biblical faith incorporates doubt into the life of faith. Doubt
receives a rather playful pose in the story of Gideon. Even though
the "spirit of the LORD had taken possession of Gideon" (Judges 6:34)
and the angel of the LORD had already been present to Gideon with
a miraculous sign, Gideon requested a further sign to make sure God
was with him as he led the Israelites into battle. The tenuousness of
Gideon's confidence is discerned in his double and contrary requests:
first the fleece of wool will have dew on it while the surrounding
floor will be dry; then the next day, the request is the opposite, just
in case (see Judges 6:36-40). Gideon wrestled with his own sense of
doubt that God was calling him to lead God's people. Gideon knew
he was on shaky ground when he said, "'Do not let your anger burn
against me'" (6:39), but he could not resist further confirmations to
deal with his own inner turmoil.

Even more pronounced examples of doubt emerge at the close of
each of the four Gospel writings. In Mark, the women at the empty
tomb are not to be alarmed and to tell the Easter message to the
disciples, but they left the tomb in fear and "said nothing to anyone"
(Mark 16:8). Thus ends the Gospel of Mark, with fear and silence

instead of confidence and speech. In Luke, the disciples hear the resurrection message from the women but receive it as "an idle tale" (Luke 24:11). The two disciples on the road to Emmaus were joined by the risen Jesus and still were slow to grasp what they were experiencing in his presence, although they later acknowledged, "Were not our hearts burning within us?" (Luke 24:32). In John, not only Thomas but also the other disciples were not jubilant until they saw the wounds of Christ. After seeing the wounds of his hands and side, "the disciples rejoiced when they saw the Lord" (John 20:20). Matthew presents one of the more dramatic endings to a Gospel. When Jesus gives the disciples what is now referred to as the Great Commission, he is speaking to his own, some of whom worshiped while others doubted as Jesus spoke to them (Matthew 28:17). Amazingly, Jesus does not cajole, correct, or reject the doubting disciples. Jesus does not send the doubting disciples back to remedial discipleship school until they get their faith straight and successfully overcome all doubts. With their mixture of worship and doubt, they are all sent into the harvest field to make other disciples. Similarly, the story of Peter's denial of Jesus exists in all four of the Gospel accounts. Doubt, fear, even denial do not thwart the work of God in the lives of the disciples.

With Gideon, the disciples of Jesus, Mother Teresa, and the cloud of witnesses throughout the ages, the biblical message endorses an understanding of the Christian faith that trusts the grace and mercy of God to stand greater and firmer than human doubts. The noted twentieth-century theologian Paul Tillich observed, "This element of doubt is a condition of all spiritual life."[4] It keeps us humble. As with the people of the Bible, it can lead us from disbelief, confusion, and inaction to trust, insight, and bold action. Doubt gives us the very experience of relying on grace. It is what makes faith, from the human perspective, an act of courage, trusting in the work of God rather than our own powers to direct and control life's events.

Where to Begin

To dare to address Christian faith, the life and work of the church, the local congregation, and the faith life of homes and individuals, one must begin with modesty, humility, the wisdom of not knowing, and, most especially, the compassion and mercy of God to be the source of any biblical faith and any real renewal for individuals, homes, congregations, and all other communities of faith in Christ. The four tips listed above provide perspectives that can help overcome typical roadblocks to congregational renewal. *From the Great Omission to Vibrant Faith* endorses leadership that pursues congregational renewal using a common language of the 6-5-4-3 with patience and perseverance and employing a commitment to create new habits—new practices in the lives of people—not just new ideas. Beneath all of this is a humble awareness of the presence of human doubt in the midst of Christian faith that requires us at all times to rely upon the mercy and the creative and redeeming work of God in Christ alone. Begin and end the journey of congregational leadership with the grace, mercy, and peace of the triune God.

Understand that the journey of faith cannot be endorsed for others if the leaders are not on the path themselves. This means the leaders need to be fluent with the Vibrant Faith Frame language, practicing the spirit of patience with themselves and others, pursuing the new habits of Christian discipleship, and being open to entering the waters of and learning from the honest and humbling experience of doubt. This way congregational leaders will make better guides and encouragers of the Christian faith in homes, congregations, and larger world. They will be leaders who are themselves authentic, available, and affirming.

7

FIND OUT

THE ROLE OF RESEARCH

Find Out!

Ongoing research is essential to the success of introducing the Vibrant Faith Frame to homes and congregations. It begins by scrutinizing one's own experiences to determine what is true and valuable as well as challenging and difficult in one's own life. It then continues by exploring how ministry efforts impact the lives of others. As a congregational coach, I routinely ask how the Vibrant Faith Frame recommendations and strategies are working for the congregation and for individual households. Repeatedly, I get the answer, "I don't know." My response to "I don't know" and to "we have no idea if the resources and ideas are actually being used" is this: "Find out!"

If we don't know the impact of the ministry of the church, we cannot know how to make a difference. It is evident that the leadership of the church, especially the congregational church, has been trained to distribute ideas and sometimes even resources. But that same leadership often has not been prepared to do the research that asks if the efforts made any difference. This is perhaps due in part to a church culture, piety, and theological orientation that do not want to question how the work and word of God are impacting people's lives. An alternative would be to endorse a church culture, piety, and theological orientation that see human hands and feet and voices as part of the very work of the Holy Spirit to make a difference in the lives of people. If we are free to train people how to preach and lead worship better at seminaries and workshops, we need to be free to help people evaluate their efforts in every other area of ministry to make sure all efforts do a better job of transforming lives.

The research needed is relational research, that is, research that connects with and deepens existing relationships in the life of the congregation and the life of family, friends, and acquaintances. For example, when a faith formation event like first communion class has been conducted, an essential part of the game plan is the follow-up interviews. Evaluation forms distributed at the end of an event that seek to learn what was and was not helpful need to be standard pieces in a congregation's life. But those forms do not tell leaders how the event actually impacted the lives of the participants weeks or months later. Whether it is a Bible study, mission trip, or a Milestone Ministry event like a first communion class or one that equips and blesses new drivers and their drivers' licenses, it is important to learn how the event impacted lives and relationships and how it can impact faith-forming relationships even more in the future.

> " It is important for leaders to find out what the Vibrant Faith Frame really looks like in daily lives. "

Implications for Congregational Leadership

A congregational leadership model that values spiritual care (paying attention to the faith formation happening in people's lives) and organizational direction (making sure that people's gifts do not get separated into silos but rather work toward the common good with a common vision and mission in the congregation), has vast implications as congregations move more fully into the direction of the Vibrant Faith Frame. First, it implies that research be conducted regularly to learn how the Vibrant Faith Frame is impacting lives. This research can be as simple as checking in with others to see how the 6-5-4-3 is a part of their lives.

Those who introduce the Vibrant Faith Frame to a congregation would be wise to begin by paying attention to their own lives. It fits under the motto of "practice what you preach." That point needs to be made regularly. Since faith is caught more than it is taught, it is important to learn by the experience of living the Four Keys consciously in one's own life. It allows the leaders to experience the challenge of practicing any discipline in our stressful and demanding world. It also allows for leaders to experience the beauty, joy, and peace that passes understanding through caring conversations, devotions, service, and rituals and traditions. The Four Keys need to be practiced cross+generationally to promote meaningful and trusted relationships.

It is important for leaders to find out what the Vibrant Faith Frame really looks like in daily lives. As one parish pastor put it after being coached for a year in the Vibrant Faith Frame,

> *I have gained an appreciation for the Four Keys. Due to conscious observation in my own life, I can now see how these Four Keys are active on a daily basis. I have learned that "service" does not have to be a service project but is evident in the daily fulfilling of the vocations God has given me. I especially see this in the simple and sometimes not so simple service of caring for my infant son. I am not only serving him and my wife, but I am serving the Lord in fulfilling the vocation of father. I have learned that rituals and traditions take time to establish, but they really show what you hold to be important in your life. For me, it is family time and the quality of that time together. The tradition of making the sign of the cross upon my son's*

head as he lays down to sleep, and the tradition of saying the words, "the Lord be with you," to my wife and son each day as I walk out the door have become a mainstay in our household. I have learned that devotions are the foundation of our time together as a family because it is the word of God that grounds us each day. I have learned that caring conversations, though a struggle for me at times, are essential to my wife feeling loved and having a "full love tank" (The Five Love Languages). I know that in all of these Four Keys, it is not only essential to recognize, to name and claim them each day but also not to hold on to them myself. It is essential to pass them on to those that I work with so that those Four Keys can be named and claimed by them. These Keys provide a contagious method of living the faith intentionally on a daily basis.

It is evident that this pastor learned to value the Four Keys as he lived them intentionally in his own home. He concluded that the Four Keys "provide a contagious method of living the faith intentionally on a daily basis." The pastor or other congregational leader who leads with this conviction is one who will more easily convey this to others and excite others to live the Vibrant Faith Frame. His story gives a good example of how the lives of the leaders become valuable laboratories for research that guides their own teaching and leading by wondering how God is at work in their lives as well as how God might be at work in the lives of others.

The Vibrant Faith Frame cannot be real for others if it is not real for those who promote it. As one pastor said after being coached in the 6-5-4-3 frame for a year, "This ministry will not be real for the congregation until it is real for me. I want to start by trying out the Four Keys in my own home, reading the *Frogs without Legs* book with my wife. After that I want the staff to do the same in their own homes. Then we will be ready to teach it to the council and larger congregation." This pastor understood not only the concepts but the application that begins with the leaders.

Of course, one need not be married or have children as in the two examples above to bring the Vibrant Faith Frame into one's own home and daily life experiences. One pastor who has followed the work of TYFI over the years and done an excellent job teaching it to congregations provided the following account of her own life as a single adult. A close scrutiny of her story will reveal that all of the Four Keys are present.

> *As a single person, the godchildren in my life are especially important to me. At one time, I lived just down the street from a godson, Andrew, from his birth until he was seven years old. He and his family and I shared many meal times together, as well as other times of play and reading and general fun. I was amazed at how quickly ritual becomes important in the life of even the youngest children. Meal times were begun and ended with prayer—some of them boisterous, some of them quiet, some spoken, some sung, some involving our whole bodies. His parents and I also told Bible stories, and my godson learned those quickly. I remember especially a time when his father had taught the children the story of Noah and the flood. About a week later Andrew, then about four, reported out to me that there were three floods in that story: the flood of people's evil, the flood of water, and the flood of God's love. He remembered this from his parents' teaching. Deep bonding takes place in all that. Even though he and I now live a long way from each other, when we are able to be together it is as familiar and easy as if we were still on the same street.*

From the mealtime rituals to devotions to service through sharing a meal together, playing, and reading to and with a child to caring conversations between a godmother and a godchild, all of the Four Keys contributed to the faith and family bond that held them together in God's love. No wonder this single adult and pastor was such a good proponent and teacher of the Vibrant Faith Frame to others.

Checking in with Others: A Form of Soft Research

Jesus used a similar form of making disciples with his own inner circle before sending them out to evangelize the world. He did not begin with a curriculum or a program for his followers to recite and memorize but a way of life that engaged his followers with daily life experiences and conversations. This method was filled with opportunities to check in with his followers (soft research) to affirm and correct their understandings and behavior. However, in today's congregational life too often God's word is preached and taught and then the people are sent out with a spirit of, "Good luck, hope something happens." But Jesus not only proclaims, he engages those with whom he spoke and worked with conversations, questions, and challenges.

In Matthew 16:13-23 Jesus questions his own disciples on how others understand who he is. He also questions his disciples on what they think. Peter seems to get it when he says, "'You are the Messiah, the son of the living God'" (Matthew 16:16). But then Peter rebuked Jesus for Jesus' statements about Jesus' own future. It does not fit with Peter's understanding of Messiah. Peter had the right language but the wrong definition of the kind of messiah Jesus represented. It was finally Jesus who had to rebuke Peter.

This is not so different from generations of Christians who use certain words and phrases with each other yet never realize how differently they understand those terms. When and how do congregational leaders check in with each other to explore more deeply what they are saying and how it is understood by one another? In Mark 10:35-45, Jesus' disciples once again have to learn what it means to be his followers and what it means to be first in his reign. It is quite different than many would suspect, but without active conversation that checks in with one another's views, Jesus would never be able to clarify or truly present his unique ministry to the world. Jesus not only gives us the message and hope for all time but the method of expanding this realm to the ends of the earth.

Once the Vibrant Faith Frame is being used by leaders, it needs to be discussed, supported, and questioned by those consciously using it. Here is where the spiritual care takes place by checking in with one another in homes, on staff, and in other leadership teams like councils, boards, sessions, and vestries. How is it going as an individual consciously uses the Four Keys in one's own life? What seems so natural? What is difficult? Where do people need help from one another in the community of faith? For example, when a council president scoffs and says that he could not expect his own family to practice the Four Keys for ten minutes a week (an actual situation reported by a pastor), it may say more about the president's home life and faith than it does about the Four Keys. That president needs the spiritual care of the pastor or some other trusted caregiver to help the president wonder about the role of faith in his daily life as well as the role of his leadership in the congregation. What is being led? What is "the business of the church" over which the president is presiding? What specifically prevents the president from engaging in faith practices for a few minutes with his own family? This is also important research to be conducted. Instead of being disappointed or threatened by the president's resistance, let the president's own needs be the focus of the learning of the Four Keys and Five Principles so that a AAA president can emerge.

The Using, Abusing, and Losing Syndrome

Caring for the needs of the president through a caring conversation that includes exploratory and personal questions in the example above also gets to the heart of what debilitates congregational leadership. Instead of caring for the leaders by investigating how their experience in congregational leadership is going, the church tends to use, abuse, and then lose valued lay leaders. Staff members are often so pleased and relieved that people are willing to take on some of the leadership responsibility that staff at times do not think of how to care for these people who give of their time. Being on a church governing board, council, or vestry sets one up as a likely candidate to be an inactive member of the congregation in the future. Instead of using, abusing, and losing those willing leaders, energies need to be put into their own survival and thriving in the Christian faith.

Leaders join governing bodies with hopes, expectations, and dreams, some of which do not come to pass. They end their terms at times with great joy for the journey, others with great joy that it is over. A pastor who understands her or his role as a spiritual caregiver will check in with the governing leaders during their term. (Let's be realistic. If the pastor checks in at least once, she or he is doing well.). When the term of office is over, check in again with caring conversation regarding the experience, a devotional that wonders how God was part of the term, serving the leader by giving that person the dignity of offering the spiritual care, and the tradition of doing the visit and the ritual of absolution for that which did not go well and thanksgiving for that which did. This kind of pastoral care will keep more retired leaders in the life of the congregation and the Vibrant Faith Frame for years to come.

Using, abusing, and losing leaders (read "servants") is not limited to governing boards. Juanita was the congregation's hostess for funerals, weddings, and anniversary celebrations at Cross of Glory. She did her assignment—her ministry—with delight and zeal, even though there were many times she had no idea how many people to plan for and how to get enough help in the church kitchen. She did this for years as an elder of the congregation, but at age eighty she and her husband moved. At their last worship service at Cross of Glory, the pastor publicly named her replacement, giving the replacement high praise for the person's willingness to serve and dedication to the ministry of the congregation. Juanita never looked for or expected a word of thanks, but she left that day unable to ignore the contrast between the pastor's praise for her successor and silence at her own faithful, dedicated service over the years.

The pastor committed the using-abusing-and-losing syndrome. He thanked Juanita's successor in no small way to say, "Thank God I don't have to worry about that troublesome assignment anymore. I doubted we would find someone as dedicated and as good as Juanita, but at least we have someone! Thanks be to God I don't have to worry about that for a while." His exuberant praise for Juanita's successor may have been more about his relief than anything else. And Juanita walks away from the congregation a little confused and perhaps a little disappointed, although she never expected public recognition in the first place. Spiritual care includes genuine words of thanks as well as sense of relief. If the pastor had even occasionally checked in with Juanita over the years to learn of the difficulties and the anxieties about having enough food and servers to care for the groups, perhaps he would have been more appreciative and communicated that appreciation to her along the way.

Check in with Staff

Of course, it is not just appointed or elected leaders, those who willingly give of their time and efforts without pay, who need to be interviewed and occasionally checked in with. I have worked with more than one pastor, youth and family director, or Christian education director who has been on the receiving end of the using-abusing-and-losing syndrome. This is especially true when staff members are seeking to move forward with the Vibrant Faith Frame while others in the congregation resist. Boards, councils, and elders need to be aware that sometimes staff leaders outgrow their former self understanding and are ready and willing to take on new tasks and role identities. Unfortunately, some staff members have felt that their congregations would not let them grow in their field or develop new ways of serving in the congregation.

When pastors discover that they are more than paid workers but are also equippers for others to engage in ministry, when youth and family directors realize the cross+generational nature of their work that includes more than just the parents of the youth, and when Christian education directors become more excited about faith formation than the next Sunday school curriculum, too often they are restricted from acting on these new insights and passions. It is difficult for congregations to let staff members grow into a more developed understanding of their ministry. People become content with their staff leaders and feel threatened when those leaders want to grow and develop their leadership in new ways.

It is well advised that non-staff leaders check in with staff to make sure their passions, interests, and growth are not ignored at the expense of the status quo. It is a sad thing for congregations to lose beloved pastors and other staff simply because the congregation was not aware of or willing to accept the need for the growth of their own staff members. Here are some questions to ask staff and non-staff leaders annually.

What excites you about your ministry in the congregation?

What would you list as some of your accomplishments this past year?

How is your ministry contributing to the vision and mission of the congregation?

How is the congregation contributing to your own sense of vision and mission?

What would help you do an even more effective job this next year?

How have you grown in your ministry this past year?

In what areas of your ministry would you like to see personal growth in the future?

In what areas of your ministry would you like to see congregational growth?

What else should we know to be of support to your ministry in the congregation?

What else should we know to be of support to your discipleship in your home and daily life?

These kinds of questions can avoid misunderstandings and disappointments on the part of leaders as well as the larger congregation. These questions confront the using-abusing-and-losing syndrome. The transparency offered through such questions and answers can spur new motivation and excitement for both individual leaders and the larger congregational community. The church is always motivated by God's future, not complacency or contentment. As Jesus said, "No one who puts a hand to the plow and looks back is fit for the kingdom of God" (Luke 9:62).

> People become content with their staff leaders and feel threatened when those leaders want to grow and develop their leadership in new ways.

Research with a Vibrant Faith Task Force

A Vibrant Faith Task Force would be a good means to conduct congregational research, that is, a means to check in with people in the congregation to determine how ministry is developing through the Vibrant Faith Frame. The task force makes sure that the efforts of the congregation do not turn the 6-5-4-3 frame into another program that is tried for a year or two then abandoned for the next latest and greatest program.

Members of the task force become the guinea pigs who allow their lives and those of their friends and families to experiment with the Four Keys in their daily lives, report back on the benefits and challenges, and encourage more of the congregation to move forward with the Vibrant Faith Frame. The task force should have about six to eight members representing at least three generations in the life of the congregation, both genders, and a liaison from the staff. The task force will want to include visionary people who get the "big picture," action-step people who can work the details, and stakeholders, those for whom this ministry truly needs to work.

The purpose of the Vibrant Faith Task Force is to inspire, envision, and advocate for change that embraces the church within the home and the congregation and nurtures a cross+generational Christian faith community. That happens best when the task force sees itself as a learning and evaluative team that checks in with people to see how ideas for faith formation, especially the Four Keys, are being lived by individuals, homes, and congregational teams. The task force should Four Key its own meetings (name and use caring conversations, devotions, service, and rituals and traditions) and promote the use of the Four Keys in the daily lives of its members. This way the homes of the task force members become living laboratories and sources of vital information and inspiration.

Beyond its own members, the Vibrant Faith Task Force should identify staff, other congregational leaders, and new members as the people to support, train, and encourage in the Christian life endorsed by the Vibrant Faith Frame. A pivotal way of targeting these strategic groups is to interview them to learn about their needs, passions, gifts, and how the Vibrant Faith Frame impacts those needs, passions, and gifts. Interviewing people identifies roadblocks that deter people from engaging more actively in the Vibrant Faith Frame.

Five Benefits of Interview Research

Doing interviews in person, by phone, or through the Internet does several significant things in the life of the congregation. First, it values the contributions of participants. This works marvelously to motivate their future participation and interest in the ministry of the congregation. It tells the participants that their insights and contributions matter. It serves as an example of the leadership adage, "People support what they help create." Once the leaders have learned from the participants, then the participants feel they have helped create something new and are more likely to want to support it in the future.

Secondly, interviewing people and evaluating ministry events values the material being studied. It makes a statement that this topic is deeply important to the ministry of the congregation and the larger church, including the church in the home. Doing research markets valued ministry. It points out to people that this ministry is worth paying attention to. A pastor, Christian education director, youth director, task force member, or any other servant leader in the congregation who does research by contacting others has just made a powerful statement about the ministry of the congregation and the participation of others in it.

Third, doing research on the various ministries of the congregation gives new data and insight to those who plan the worship or the study or the trip. All of that contributes to a better experience in the future. It also offers insights and suggestions that can be communicated to others through sermons, Bible studies, newsletters, websites, leadership meetings, and simple conversations.

Fourth, doing follow up research itself teaches. It provides a redundant message, helping people recall what they experienced and what they learned. All that deepens the initial experience through the second experience of reflecting and evaluating what impacted people's lives.

Finally, doing research enriches the life of the community. It promotes a congregational life that is less hierarchical and more mutual. It lifts up the priesthood of all believers, the priesthood of all contributors to the work of the church. People value being valued. They want to be part of communities that understand the importance of God gifting others besides those leading and making decisions for the whole. Research creates a positive feeling and sense of commitment to the mission of the congregation and larger church.

Of course, the critical element in all of these benefits is taking the research seriously and communicating to the larger community how the information will be used in the future. People resent being toyed with to give information that will not be used in any significant way. The benefits are real, but if the research is not handled with integrity, so are the disappointments.

One pastor conducted research on a new resource handed out in worship services. The congregation had begun to use the Taking Faith Home[1] bulletin insert that provides Four Key ideas and numerous Bible passages to be used in the home each week. The pastor asked the following simple and direct questions:

> Do you know that the Taking Faith Home (TFH) resource is in the bulletin each week?
> Do you take it home and use it?
> If you do use TFH, what part(s) do you use?
> How often do you use TFH? (circle one of the following: daily, three or more times a week, weekly, a couple times a month, monthly, less than once a month)
> What have you found helpful in the TFH resource?
> What other information would be helpful for your congregation to know about TFH?

The pastor conducted the research by randomly emailing fifteen households each month. One particular month ten responded. He learned that everyone who responded was aware of the Taking Faith Home resource. He also gained a great story and example of how one family used it to connect with children and grandchildren. He also learned how the respondents tended to value it more than they used it. One respondent was waiting for "divine intervention" to get that person actually to use it, suggesting the need for help in creating a new discipline, a new habit in one's daily life. Some who did not use Taking Faith Home informed the pastor that they used other similar devotional resources. All of this became data that informed his preaching, teaching, and overall pastoral leadership in the congregation. It marketed the resource with fifteen households each month. It valued the resource enough to get responses from people about it. The emails gave insight as to how the resource was being used and motivation to give further help to people in using it.

> " Do less, not more, just do it more thoroughly, that is, go deeper. "

Do Less, but Do It More Thoroughly

A fundamental recommendation for Vibrant Faith congregations is to do less, not more, just do it more thoroughly, that is, go deeper. Research represents an added element to the ministry of many congregations, congregations where servant leaders often feel overwhelmed as it is. The Vibrant Faith Frame will not promote vibrant faith if people end up exhausted and feeling guilty for not doing enough. The goal is not overworked, underappreciated servant leaders. Church and society have already reinforced a view that being busy is the goal and primary value in life.

The other two books in the Vibrant Faith series offer a number of examples and ideas that have been tried in congregations and in homes. They serve as suggestions to consider and stimulation for numerous variations to create for your own home and congregational contexts. In the midst of all these ideas and possible activities, it can easily be imagined that the reader becomes more burdened than relieved as one considers all the options.

Instead, it is hoped that the options and possibilities give new energy as to how one engages in the ministries of our congregations across the country. When it comes to worship and preaching, pastors and other worship leaders are already committed to planning time. Christian education already occurs regularly. Youth group activities happen occasionally or regularly, and annual fellowship activities are anticipated even before they are listed on congregational calendars. The suggestions offered are not to add more work but to do one's current work with the Vibrant Faith Frame in mind.

The ideas described in the Vibrant Faith series begin in typical areas of congregational ministry and home life and screen them through the Vibrant Faith Frame. The examples come from real life ministry in real congregations and homes across the country. They are not presented to dictate what must happen in any particular congregation or home. Through a team of leaders guided by the Vibrant Faith Frame, the examples can stimulate thinking, ideas, and strategies that can be utilized in any particular setting. The Frame becomes a way of thinking through and imagining what is the most effective way of doing ministry in your congregation and homes.

The fundamental premise for all of the contributions is not a list of ideas to help congregational servant leaders get through another year of programs to satisfy annual goals, numbers, and evaluative teams. The premise is to do only that which matters, only that which nurtures the Christian faith by the power of the Holy Spirit and for the needs of individuals, homes, congregations, communities, cultures, and creation itself.

To that end, do less, not more, just do it more thoroughly. That is, a congregation's activities need to be done not just because the congregation has always done it that way or just to finish a task and move on to the next. "Do less" means placing a premium on doing only that which will make a difference according to the standard of "faith working through love" (Galatians 5:6). Do only that which blesses lives with faith, hope, and love in Christ. "Do it more thoroughly" means value the ministry effort enough to do more to reinforce the desired outcome of the event. Study the impact of the congregation's efforts in the lives of individuals and homes. Explore how it might impact lives more completely. Find ways to reinforce the impact of the congregational event with helpful follow-up so that it goes deep into the flesh and bones of people. Do what is possible to ensure that the transforming power of the event is sustained over time.

"Do less, but do it more thoroughly" suggests that congregations find ways to repeat the learning for faith and life. The experience should not be forgotten or remembered as something "nice" or "fantastic" but should impact people's lives over time. This means there may be fewer events promoted on the congregation's calendar or scheduled by a family. The events that are scheduled and do happen will be supported with follow-up gatherings, research, and reflection that help people continue to wonder and explore how the message of the gospel and the Christian life makes a claim on people's lives and the world they live in from day to day.

CONCLUSION

LEADING A RENEWAL
OF THE CHURCH

This book has been written in the service of leaders who are pursuing church renewal by partnering the ministry of the congregation with the ministry of the life of faith in the home. The "home" is more broadly understood as the life of faith in and through people's daily life relationships, especially those established over time. Granted, this focus on the church in the home and the partnership of home and congregation in ministry is not the only agenda for the renewal of the church, but it is an important element that needs attention today.

Leadership for the renewing of the people of God is a humbling experience, just ask people like Abraham and Sarah, Moses, Jeremiah, Mary the mother of Jesus, Peter, Paul, and a host of others in the Bible or in the history of the church. Such leadership involves resistance, confusion, questions, doubts, and discouragement as well as hope, confidence, joy, and faith. Today, congregational leaders play an important role in the ongoing mission to renew the life of the church, not only to lift up the vision of the church's recovery from the Great Omission but of living that vision. The bottom line: Congregations cannot expect to be very effective promoting and implementing the Vibrant Faith Frame if the leaders do not incorporate the 6-5-4-3 into their own lives, especially as they practice the Four Keys in their homes, in daily life experiences, and in their leadership in the congregation.

Leaders are to apply the Vibrant Faith Frame in the two primary settings of home and congregation. It means honoring one's own home as holy ground, the church in a domestic setting. In and through one's own home (and the homes of others), leaders invest in the care of congregational life, community, culture, and creation. Leaders are encouraged to live the Four Key faith practices in the Six Locations of Ministry with the Five Principles in mind, principles that point out that faith is a relational experience, that the church is more than a congregational location and activities, that home is a valued place for the people of God to be the church (where faith is caught, not just taught), and that if we want Christian children and youth, they need to be surrounded by a host of Christian adults, mentoring, caring, and serving alongside them. All of this is directed toward Christian discipleship that is authentic, available to serve all things God has created, and affirming of the power of the gospel to save lives and redeem all of creation.

> Congregational leaders play an important role in the ongoing mission to renew the life of the church.

The second way for congregational leaders (read "servants") to appropriate the Vibrant Faith Frame is to use it as a foundational reference point in the life of the congregation itself. That means being aware of how subtly—even insidiously—the Great Omission can be communicated in a congregation, as subtle as insinuating that parents and other caregivers are primarily chauffeurs and chaperones instead of faith mentors and apostles. It means that public gatherings like worship, fellowship time, and team meetings are planned with the Four Keys in mind to nurture the Christian faith. That includes the intent to equip people with the Four Keys in those public, congregational settings so that people can apply the faith practices in their daily routines more consciously.

Congregational occasions like worship, Bible study, mission trips, and council meetings create opportunities to send people home with suggested caring conversations to have with others, Scriptures to read and pray, service ideas to commit to, and rituals and traditions to use that remind people of who and whose they are as baptized children of God in Christ. Applying the Vibrant Faith Frame in the congregation requires that the leadership attend to more than making sure the bills are paid, committees meet, and staff are doing their jobs. The business of the church is more than treating congregational operations solely like a business. It implies that congregational leaders have an identity as spiritual elders, people who are deeply committed to the Christian faith being the centerpiece of people's identity, thoughts, and conduct.

Finally, to offer effective congregational leadership under the guidance of the Vibrant Faith Frame involves attention to the kinds of issues identified and addressed in chapters 4 through 7. In a recent coaching conversation with a youth and family ministry team, a typical frustration was aired with a question from Deb, the chairperson of the team: "Besides using a blow torch, how do you fire up the people? Too many of them just don't come to our cross+generational opportunities, including Milestones Ministry. The ones who come love it, but so many others look at you with an odd stare when you invite them to a Milestone event or a cross+generational Sunday school hour. They have no idea of how it is important to their lives." Deb then noted that the children and the older adults are those most likely to get it, show up, and be enthusiastic, but many of the Baby Boomers and adults a bit younger tend to shy away.

The "blow torch" image gave clear indication of Deb's (and the team's) frustrations, that humbling experience of congregational leadership with people not quite on board. The question provided an opportunity to name the same themes presented in this book. It truly can be frustrating to have a passion for Christian discipleship through strategies like Milestones Ministry, cross+generational Sunday school hours, and the dissemination of the Four Keys back into people's daily lives and then have people stare at you like you are speaking in a foreign language. The problem is, you are speaking a foreign language. Any language that suggests participation in the life of faith beyond pew sitting and signing a pledge card can be nerve wracking to some if not to many.

The youth and family team was reminded that parents, grandparents, and other adults have not necessarily been honored over recent decades for their vital roles as Christian disciples. They can be overwhelmed and intimidated by the suggestion that they have a part to play in the faith formation of children, youth, and even other adults. During the coaching session, we discussed the need to continue to use the language of the Vibrant Faith Frame so that greater fluency with the words and concepts could develop. We talked about the need to be patient and yet persistent, because that is how fluency with any language develops. We discussed how to start with those who are present and enthusiastic, about getting their stories out into the congregation regarding how the Four Keys and the rest of the Vibrant Faith Frame are impacting lives. This is all part of the process to help those who seem to prefer to stand on the sidelines to begin intentionally practicing the Four Keys and creating new habits in their lives.

The team was reminded of the importance of doing research on what is happening in the lives of those who are participating and then getting that positive message out to others. A discussion ensued on how to connect more closely with the church council, describing the frustrations to the council members and asking for their input and help. That way, the council could own some of the concern and be encouraged to practice the Four Keys, get to know more children and youth themselves, and commit to be those who explore how Milestones and cross+generational Sunday school events can be a meaningful part of their congregational experience. The strategy was to start with the leaders as some of the people most likely to explore and discover the power of the Four Keys and the cross+generational life of the church in congregation and home.

It was suggested to the team that maybe Jesus was right. Instead of converting the whole world around him at once, he focused on twelve disciples, worked with them for three years, sent them out two by two to homes and towns, and over time the community of faith grew. Even the Son of God didn't get everyone on board at the same time. Imagine.

The team was also reminded of the Scripture and prayer used to open the coaching session. The Bible passage was Philippians 2:5-8, part of the Christ hymn that lifts up Jesus' humility, his serving as a slave instead of as one entitled to recognition as the Son of God. It was pointed out that as Christian disciples seek to follow him faithfully, they are to have this same attitude, this "same mind" as Christ had. The group responded well, encouraged by the example of Christ, the need to be humble, patient, and faithful in it all. With that perspective, the group was able to see beyond their frustrations and recall those whose lives—including their own—have been blessed by the congregation's attention to Christian faith formation and discipleship. It allowed them to recall the reasons why they are part of this ministry. Later, Deb wrote about the meeting,

> *In my frustration with what is working and what is not working, I really and truly seemed to bring it all into place when you told me the part that Jesus didn't get everyone on board after three years. It has been some two thousand years and he still doesn't have everyone on board. I guess that is how it may be for some people of our congregation, but the ones who do get it are diligent in their part and look forward to their time to spend with this whole life changing experience. I feel this is a worthwhile ministry. It changes our life of faith and will make it stronger if we just let God happen in our congregation and in our community. I wish everyone could feel as great as I do after spending time in this ministry.*

Deb had learned once again that being a servant of Christ can be both a humble yet exciting experience. Sometimes we all—especially those seeking to do the will of God in our congregations—need to be reminded of that, even with a little laughter about blow torches. Her pastor, who was also part of the coaching session added his thoughts following the meeting as well:

> *The transition from "what we have always done" into a more intentional and oddly enough traditional and proven method of passing faith to the next generation is difficult. In the life of our congregation, we now are dealing with a generation raised on television and immediate gratification with short attention spans and the expectation of being entertained. Yet what is needed and craved are authentic relationships. We have lost the skills in the life of the church to do these things . . . yet we can reclaim these. We are seeking to take such steps in intentional ways to help equip the congregation in making changes to personal behaviors in living out authentic faith in Jesus Christ. And it will take time. Old ships do not turn on a dime but rather take time and do a lot of wobbling and creaking as they turn, but they can turn. It will take time and continued efforts of prayer, worship and study . . . but we will make the turn.*

Promoting a vibrant faith formation that is authentic, available, and affirming is difficult without leadership, both lay and clergy, continually articulating the vision with faithful and humble patience and persistence, the kind expressed by Deb and her pastor. It takes a cross+generational faith community in homes and congregations to equip lives for the ministry of Christian faith formation, discipleship, and outreach to God's larger world. It is a humbling ministry in many ways. It is also filled with the light and glory of God in Christ to transform lives and relationships. It is the church in homes, congregations, and larger world that sings, prays, preaches, and teaches "that at the name of Jesus every knee should bend, in heaven and on earth and under the earth, and every tongue should confess that Jesus Christ is Lord, to the glory of God the Father" (Philippians 2:10-11).

The book ends as it began, with a word of modesty. Overcoming the Great Omission is not the only important message for the church to hear today, it is just the message consistently overlooked. For those who have recognized the faith life of the home through the ministry of the congregation, the joy has been real. It has also created a sense of call and a sense of urgency for the sake of individuals, homes, congregations, communities, cultures, and world to receive the grace, mercy, and peace of God for all that God has created and redeemed in Christ Jesus. Come Holy Spirit, renew us, renew your church again today.

ACKNOWLEDGMENTS

Writing *From the Great Omission to Vibrant Faith* was dependent upon years of work at The Youth & Family Institute, especially in the role of guest speaker, coach, and congregational trainer. In recent years that work has taken on a particular focus with specific judicatories in the church. A word of thanks must be extended to the working relationship that has developed between the North Carolina Synod and the Northwest Synod of Wisconsin, both of the Evangelical Lutheran Church in America, and TYFI. Those more recent working relationships opened doors for coaching and training to congregations, pastors, and other leaders that provided rich material explored in this book.

A special word of thanks to the following leaders in the North Carolina Synod and Northwest Synod of Wisconsin for their level of dedication to and insight, stories, and feedback regarding the Vibrant Faith Frame as the book was being conceived and written: Tim Glenham, John Mouritsen, Greg Williams, Ken Langsdorf, Ellen Koester, Gary Weant, Rebbeca Cloninger, Richard Rhoades, Deb Trautman, Tammy Jones West, Mary Toufar, Russ Sorensen, Jeff Elmquist, Carole

DeJardin, Randy Olson, Paula Davis, Darrell Kyle, and Mike Pancoast. Others whose contributions through stories and examples for this book were helpful beyond these two synods include Mark Asleson, Andrea Fieldhouse, Adam Gless, Julie Miller, Paul Nelson, and Lucas Woodford.

Of course, many others have communicated their ideas and encouragement to continue down this particular road toward renewing the life of faith in homes, congregations, and the larger church. In addition to the innumerable and unnamed contributors, two groups of people are important to mention. The first is a group of ecumenical church leaders whose guidance was instrumental to the development of the language of the Vibrant Faith Frame, language that would move TYFI beyond the confines of youth and family ministry to the larger arena of congregational renewal and adult faith formation. They include Dawn Alitz, TYFI associate; Rhonda Hanisch, senior pastor at Ascension Lutheran Church in Brookings, S.D.; Lisa Kimball, professor at Virginia Theological Seminary in Alexandria, Va.; Paul Nelson, senior pastor at Immanuel Lutheran Church in Eden Prairie, Minn.; John Roberto, president of LifelongFaith Associates in Naugatuck, Conn.; Chip Stokes, Rector at St. Paul's Episcopal Church in Delray Beach, Fla.; Amy Scott Vaughn, previously a director of the Institute for Youth Ministry at Princeton Theological Seminary; and Larry Wagner, senior pastor at Ascension Lutheran Church in Thousand Oaks, Calif. Their wisdom, guidance, and encouragement came at a pivotal moment in the life of TYFI. They have significantly influenced the current direction of the Institute to embrace the language and strategies of the Vibrant Faith Frame and Ministries. Thank you for your partnership in ministry.

Another group of committed people were instrumental to the final edition of this book. They include three readers of the manuscript whose personal investment in the writing project is evident from the fact that each contributed their own stories: Dick Bruesehoff, Greg Kaufmann, and Stephanie Frey. They read, critiqued, cheered, and challenged the manuscript into becoming a better contribution for the life of the church. Their passionate efforts and support are seen in the final edition of the book.

A deep word of appreciation to the TYFI family, staff, associates, board, and friends of the Institute whose passion, dedication, leadership, and faith have kept this vision going for years across the Unites States and sometimes beyond. Bill Huff and Josh Messner, who served as project director and editor respectively, offered valuable insights and skill to the development of the manuscript and to the final text and look of the book. A special word of thanks to our executive director, Paul Hill, whose guidance and support to write this book and the larger Vibrant Faith series were critical to the accomplishment of the writing project.

APPENDIX

BIBLICAL REFERENCES FOR THE SIX, FIVE, FOUR, THREE

SIX LOCATIONS OF MINISTRY:
GOD'S ACTIVITY IN ALL THE WORLD

1. Children and youth: Isaiah 11:6; Mark 10:13-16; 1 Timothy 4:11-16

2. Homes: Mark 1:29-34; Colossians 4:15; Philemon 1-2

3. Congregations: Galatians 1:1-2; Philippians 1:1; 2 John 1-2

4. Community: Mark 1:38-39; Luke 19:1-10; Acts 18:1-4

5. Culture: Psalm 105-106; Isaiah 45:1-8; Acts 17:22-31

6. Creation: Genesis 1-2; Psalm 104; Matthew 6:26-30

THE FIVE PRINCIPLES: ELEMENTS OF A VIBRANT CHURCH

1. Faith is formed by the power of the Holy Spirit through personal trusted relationships—often in our own homes. John 1:29-51; 4:28-42; 1 Thessalonians 2:7, 11, 17; 2 John 9-12; 3 John 13-14

2. The church is a living parternship between the ministry of the congregation and the ministry of the home. Acts 2:46-47; 5:41-42; 20:20

3. Where Christ is present in faith, the home is church, too. Acts 10:24; 16:14-15, 30-34, 40; Romans 16:3-16; 1 Corinthians 16:19; Philemon 1-2

4. Faith is caught more than it is taught. Deuteronomy 6:6-9; Matthew 10:32-33 with 26:69-75

5. If we want Christian children and youth, we need Christian adults/parents. Deuteronomy 6:20-22; 11:1-2; 2 Timothy 1:5

THE FOUR KEYS: FAITH PRACTICES FOR LIVING ONE'S BAPTISM

1. Caring Conversation: Colossians 4:5-6; Matthew 21:28;
   Eccl. 3:1; James 1:19

2. Devotions: Matthew 6:7-13; Acts 2:42; Acts 12:12;
   Ephesians 5:15-20

3. Service: Isaiah 58:6-8; Mark 10:43-45; Acts 2:43-47;
   James 1:27

4. Rituals and Traditions: Joshua 4:4-7; Luke 2:41-52;
   2 Thessalonians 2:15; Revelation19:6-9

AAA ROAD SERVANT:
WHAT A CHRISTIAN DISCIPLE LOOKS LIKE

1. Authentic (1 Corinthians 4:8-17)

2. Available (Matthew 25:31-46)

3. Affirming (Philippians 1:3-11)

Notes

1. The Great Omission

1. *Leading the Team-Based Church: How Pastors and Church Staff Can Grow Together into a Powerful Fellowship of Leaders*, George Cladis (San Francisco: Jossey-Bass, 1999), 135.

2. *The Way We Never Were: American Families and the Nostalgia Trap*, Stephanie Coontz (New York: Basic, 1992).

2. The Vibrant Faith Frame

1. Christian Smith with Melinda Lundquist Denton, *Soul Searching: The Religious and Spiritual Lives of American Teenagers* (New York: Oxford University Press, 2005), 56.

2. *Ibid.*

3. *Evangelical Lutheran Worship*, 72 (emphasis mine).

4. *The Partnership for Missional Church Local Church Guide*, Pat Keifert (St. Paul: Church Innovations), 19.

5. Mark DeFries, *Family Based Youth Ministry, Revised and Expanded* (Downers Grove: InterVarsity, 2004), 15.

6. Rodney Atkins, *Watching You* video.

7. Robert Wuthnow, *Growing Up Religious: Christians and Jews and Their Journeys of Faith* (Boston: Beacon, 1999), xxxii.

8. *Ibid.*

9. Peter L. Benson and Carolyn H. Eklin, *Effective Christian Education: A National Study of Protestant Congregations* (Minneapolis: Search Institute, 1990), 38.

10. *Ibid.*

11. Gordon W. Lathrop, *The Pastor: A Spirituality* (Minneapolis: Fortress, 2006), 86.

3. The Need to Repent of the Great Omission

1. *New Rules: Searching for Self-Fulfillment in a World Turned Upside Down*, Daniel Yankelovich (New York: Random, 1981), 263.

2. *To Kill a Mockingbird*, Harper Lee (New York: HarperCollins, 1960), 19.

3. Not all the dreams for science were dashed. The work of public health programs did extend the average life expectancy by twenty-five years during the twentieth century.

4. Brigitte Birger, "The Family as a Mediating Structure," in *Democracy and Mediating Structures: A Theological Inquire*, ed. Michael Novak (Washington, D.C.: American Enterprise Institute for Public Policy Research, 1980), 145.

5. Allen H. Sager, *Gospel-Centered Spirituality: An Introduction to Our Spiritual Journey* (Minneapolis: Augsburg Fortress, 1990), 113.

6. James D. Anderson and Ezra Earl Jones, *Ministry of the Laity* (San Francisco: Harper, 1986), 62.

7. *God Is in the Small Stuff: And It All Matters*, Bruce Bickel and Stan Jantz. (Uhrichsville: Barbour: 1998), 60.

8. Cited in *A New Day for Family Ministry*, Richard P. Olson and Joe H. Leonard Jr. (New York: Alban Institute, 1996), 49–53.

9. Thursday, June 19, 2008, *Star Tribune*, Opinion, A15.

10. *Big Russ and Me: Father and Son—Lessons of Life*, Tim Russert (New York: Hyperion, 2005). Later he added a second book based on the many letters he received following *Big Russ and Me* entitled *Wisdom of Our Fathers: Lessons and Letters from Daughters and Sons* (New York: Random, 2007).

11. Email message from Rebecca Clonninger, June 2, 2008.

12. Emails from congregational member, April 6-7, 2008.

13. This is language Martin Luther used to describe parents and their role in the faith life of children. See "The Estate of Marriage" (1522), LW 45:46.

4. Understanding and Mercy for Parents and Caregivers

1. Roy W. Fairchild, "Parental Stress in Protestant Homes: Clues from Research," in *Sex, Family, and Society*, ed. John Charles Wynn (New York: Association, 1966), 101.

2. "The Estate of Marriage" (1522), *LW* 45:46.

3. Martin Luther, *Sermons on the Gospel*, trans. E. Schmid and D. M. Martens, vol. 1 (Rock Island: Augustana, 1871), vii.

4. Richard H. Bliese and Craig Van Gelder, eds., *The Evangelizing Church: A Lutheran Contribution* (Minneapolis: Augsburg Fortress, 2005), 82.

5. See example of this in *Frogs without Legs Can't Hear: Nurturing Disciples in Home and Congregation* (Minneapolis: Augsburg, 2003), 49-50.

6. Kristen Venne, *The Family as the Center of Faith Formation: A Study of the Connection between Home and Congregation in the Faith Lives of Families in Congregations Implementing the Child In Our Hands Initiative,* thesis submitted to the faculty of Luther Seminary, St. Paul, MN, 2007, 106–7.

7. Email correspondence from Andrea Fieldhouse, July 9, 2008.

8. FaithTalk cards are produced by TYFI and are intended to promote caring conversations in daily life. The cards are especially helpful for families and other small group settings.

9. See the story of the spiritual life of parents in *Frogs without Legs Can't Hear*, 14.

10. Martin E. Marty, *The Mystery of the Child* (Grand Rapids: Eerdmans, 2007).

11. The *Taking Faith Home* resource from TYFI is a bulletin insert that is to be taken home by the worshippers. It is filled with Four Key suggestions, Scripture readings, prayers, blessings, and thoughts to meditate on throughout the week.

5. The Business of the Church

1. William M. Easum, *Sacred Cows Make Gourmet Burgers: Ministry Anytime, Anywhere, by Anyone* (Nashville: Abingdon, 1995), 9.

2. See www.exemplarym.com.

3. *For Everything There Is a Season* is a resource that gives numerous Four Key ideas that fit into the daily lives of people around specific milestones in life like a wedding or house blessing. It is written by the Nielsen family and published by TYFI.

6. Effective Leadership with the Vibrant Faith Frame

1. The Hand in Hand is a congregational training offered by TYFI introducing the congregation to the Vibrant Faith Frame. By the end of the weekend training, a critical mass of people from the congregation understand and are excited by the concepts and have identified strategic next steps to implement the Vibrant Faith Frame in home and congregation.

2. Martin Luther, Small Catechism, *The Book of Concord: The Confessions of the Evangelical Lutheran Church* (Minneapolis: Augsburg Fortress, 2000), 347–48.

3. See *Time*, "Mother Teresa's Crisis of Faith," David Van Biema, August 23, 2007.

4. Paul Tillich, *The Courage to Be* (New Haven: Yale University Press, 1952), 48.

7. Find Out: The Role of Research

1. Greg Priebbenow, *Taking Faith Home* (Youth & Family Institute, www.tyfi.org).

Books by David W. Anderson
arriving in 2010 and 2011

Vibrant Faith in the Congregation gives congregational leaders practical, concrete ideas of what the Vibrant Faith Frame looks like within the various ministries of a congregation. The areas of ministry explored through the Vibrant Faith Frame include worship and preaching, Christian education, youth and family ministry, evangelism, stewardship, before-school and after-school programs, buildings and grounds, and how to have a meaningful relationship to outdoor ministries within the church.

Vibrant Faith in the Home gives individuals, couples, and larger families and households practical and concrete ideas of what the Vibrant Faith Frame looks like in the home. It will include how to live the Four Keys on a daily basis and how to punctuate the Christian life in and through the home via particular milestones in people's lives as well as how to connect the home with the larger ministry of congregation, community, culture, and creation.

Both books will include narratives of how the Vibrant Faith Frame is lived in actual congregations and homes.

To order other books and resources from The Youth & Family Institute, go to www.tyfi.org or call 877-239-2492

THE VIBRANT FAITH FRAME

6 SIX LOCATIONS of ministry

- *Children and youth*
  Children and youth, recognized and empowered as disciples of Jesus Christ, use their God-given gifts in purposeful ministry.
- *Homes*
  Families are equipped and strengthened by their congregation to be the primary nurturers of faith.
- *Congregations*
  Congregations are safe, inclusive, welcoming, and nurturing for all children, youth, and adults, as they live out their faith in the midst of community and the larger world.
- *Community*
  Christians live their faith daily, experiencing Christ in Community, learning from, as well as serving the needs of community.
- *Culture*
  Children, youth, and adults experience God's presence, learning from people from a variety of Cultures, while being part of God's transformational work within culture.
- *Creation*
  Christians live in harmony with Creation, recognizing, receiving, celebrating, and caring for God's handiwork.

5 FIVE PRINCIPLES of a vibrant church

- Faith is formed by the power of the Holy Spirit through personal trusted relationships—often in our own homes.
- The church is a living partnership between the ministry of the congregation and ministry of the home.
- Where Christ is present in faith, the home is church, too.
- Faith is caught more than it is taught.
- If we want Christian children and youth, we need Christian adults.

4 FOUR KEYS for practicing faith

- Caring Conversations
- Devotions
- Service
- Rituals and Traditions

3 THREE CHARACTERISTICS of Christian disciples

- Authentic
- Available
- Affirming

OTHER BOOKS BY DAVID W. ANDERSON

Frogs without Legs Can't Hear
Nurturing Disciples in Home and Congregation
David W. Anderson and Paul G. Hill

Comparing church to a frog?
It might seem like a crazy analogy—but beyond the comparison is a very readable book based on Scripture, research, and experience that creates a cultural shift in how faith formation is typically practiced. The theory is that it takes a whole church "frog" (the head is leadership, the torso is the congregation, and the legs are the home) to build a true Christian community and nurture faith in young people. The result is a more effective ministry that includes a stronger congregation-home partnership.

Coming of Age
Exploring the Spirituality and Identity of Younger Men
David W. Anderson, Paul G. Hill, and Roland D. Martinson

How is your church responding to the needs of a younger generation?
This book does an excellent job of identifying the issues that are important to younger men—and offers practical advice for those who minister to males in the church. Some of the topics examined include the struggles young men face as they deal with questions about relationships, work and vocation, and spirituality. This book is strongly recommended for those pastors or lay people who wish to reach out to young men and keep them strongly connected to their Christian faith.

To order other books and resources from The Youth & Family Institute, go to www.tyfi.org or call 877-239-2492